WHILE AMERICA WORKS

How Government Handles Our Affairs

John S. Davies

WHILE AMERICA WORKS

How Government Handles Our Affairs

DISCLAIMER

Although the author and publisher have made every effort to ensure the accuracy and completeness of information contained in this book, we assume no responsibility for errors, inaccuracies, omissions, or any inconsistency herein. Any slights of people, places, or organizations are unintentional.

ISBN-13: 978-1499761412

ISBN-10: 1499761414

JDF Publications
c/o The JDavies Company
2220 Otay Lakes Rd. Suite #502-211
Chula Vista, CA 91915

First printing 2014

Cover Art:
www.specialforcesartdepartment.com

DEDICATION

This goes out to all the hard working Americans who entrust the handling of their affairs to those we place in government.

INTRODUCTION

I'm an independent so I am all over the political map. Nothing can be assumed with me. Some of these commentaries are not political (most of them are) but rather general in nature. I have also included personal essays which may interrupt the flow. Some of the articles are dated as you will recognize but it doesn't in any way diminish the crux of the article. While reading I will ask you to keep in mind that America is you and I while Government is a collection of people we hire through our vote to handle our affairs "while America works" and that is what carries the weight of the message.

Anyway I hope you enjoy a mostly disjointed, but hopefully engaging, collection of commentaries.

WHILE AMERICA WORKS

How Government Handles Our Affairs

A PERSONAL NOTE

We voice our opinions in many different ways whether it be at the family dinner table or the water cooler at work or in a drunken stupor in the local watering hole. But who is listening to us? The behavior of today's politicians tell me it isn't them. No matter the differences among us we must band together in order to keep a government that seems hell bent on absolute control, from having that absolute control. It's like they are committing tyranny in an acceptable way.

These commentaries were borne out of frustration with a system that is clearly broken to all except, apparently, the people who operate it. We toil each day and give a large portion of the dollars earned to a government that is charged with spending those dollars to protect our way of life. Unfortunately, it doesn't always happen that way. Too often dollars are spent and laws created that are quite the opposite of what we expected. The only way we can keep this runaway train from leaving its tracks is to always remain vigilant in our efforts to keep our government in check.

John S. Davies

WHILE AMERICA WORKS

How Government Handles Our Affairs

CONTENTS

AT WHAT PRICE?

Another day passes in the Middle East. An American science teacher working in Benghazi is gunned down in the street while taking his morning jog. Also today, the American taxpayer will provide, to that area and the rest of the Middle East, money to do who knows what because nobody really knows. Maybe it bought the gun the American teacher was killed with? That is in no way a far fetched idea. It happens all the time. Being in that area and the surrounding areas is like setting up a temporary police substation in a gang infested area to make a statement. In the case of Afghanistan temporary means twelve years and the statement fell on deaf ears.

We need to get out. The War on Terror is making the Vietnam debacle look clean and organized. I understand we have to be involved in the activities of the area because of economic interests and the quick strike capability. No country is positioned better than the United States to protect us from current and perceived enemies. We also consume large quantities of oil and so does Russia, China, India, and the list goes on. Oil in that region is cheap. We don't know that when we roll up to the pump in our American neighborhoods because a lot goes on between the oil coming out of the ground in that region and when it finally is pumped into the tank underneath your favorite gas station pump. We also buy oil from countries who hate us (Venezuela), and countries who blame us for all their problems (Mexico), and most importantly countries who want us wiped from the face of the earth (insert any number of names of Middle Eastern countries here).

I know this piece is rhetorical because we, as in you and I, have absolutely no control in these matters. And if you attempt to use the tired phrase “you can vote” you will be exposed as someone who lives beneath a rock. I am extremely limited in my understanding of the vagaries of energy consumption as it pertains to world markets and the decisions that go into positioning ourselves militarily. My world view is from the comfort of my home. What I do want is the powers to be to know is that even though our understanding is minimal (and it was designed to be that way by the powers to be) we know something is going on that isn't right. So the charge that the government operates on two fronts, the government presented to the citizens and the clandestine government that operates on the world stage, is a worthy charge. I realize it has always been that way but because of social media today we are seeing it up close and personal. With the emergence of figures like Julian Assange and Eric Snowden we get the information fast and furious. Like them or not, guys like this get their hands on vital information that is disseminated immediately through the social media.

Unfortunately, all that has happened is the information is now known to us but nothing has changed. We have a government that basically says, okay now you know so what are you going to do about it? Other nations don't like it either but don't necessarily want to ruffle the feathers of the biggest, baddest nation on the planet. They may tell us up yours but that will be the end of it. We may shut them up with an increased foreign aid allotment or fly our B-52's over their neighborhood or strike them with a few drones. In the end we come out on top. Or actually they come out on top, meaning the clandestine government and it's financiers (not the taxpayer ones but the corporate ones). How the monies move around is far beyond our comprehension. All we are left with is the knowledge that money and military might rule the day and how it all takes place is above our pay grade. We are thrown a financial bone in that we enjoy a comparatively high standard of living and we are provided security so a terrorist doesn't walk through our front door. But at what price should all this come? The government that is presented to the people allows free speech to get a message to the clandestine government. Our message would say that we know you are going to do what you believe is best (the NSA revelation confirms that) but maybe, just maybe, you ain't all that smart. Maybe the decisions you make currently are tilted a little too much in your favor and you should make some adjustments in favor of the people? A lot of you are making decisions based on pure greed. We have seen that in the 1%. To hell with the 99% when it comes to lining your pockets.

Frankly, I don't give a s**t if you are filthy rich just don't do it by hurting me. There's lots of ways to make money, that's a given. If you choose to make money in a way that hurts others then you are a POS (see Halliburton). That's like a notch below thug. Is that how you want to be remembered? If you make your money in the energy market isn't there a way to do it so you don't stroke us so much at the pump? Or are you just too f**king lazy to find out. That would make you one greedy bastard.

And on the military front there is no question it is to our advantage to be in areas throughout the world to keep the bad guys at bay. But again, can't we adjust the way we do it? After all, you take our sons and daughters (one of which is mine) and place them in situations that are so dangerous they have no chance (see Benghazi). And then you try to dismiss your f**k up with lame excuses that would be scoffed at by our local crackheads. Obama conducts wars with our children and he has never been in the military. You continually remind us of how incredibly smart you are but you continue to do stupid s**t. I'm starting to think Harvard is a Continuation school. I hear more intelligent stuff coming out of those crackheads I mentioned than I hear coming out of you Ivy League bull sh**ters. You can't keep the economy afloat, defeat terrorists, or stop crime. What the f**k is it you do?

It's obvious Obama (Harvard) can't even spell the words foreign policy let alone conduct one. Seriously, he ignores

Israel, let's Putin have center stage, and has Joe 'foot in mouth" Biden smoothing things over in China? Obama stays here to implement his socialist policies while the Chinese are putting Biden through a kangaroo court. What's Biden's next stop, North Korea? You can't make this stuff up. Hollywood is intent on producing movies and weekly series making the conservatives look foolish when all along they have the liberals providing endless amounts of material for reality shows. They could make more money clowning their own people. It's like the mother lode of comedic material. But this stuff going on in the world right now is nothing to laugh at. The instability we see is in large part due to decisions made by the Administration and Congress. The rich and powerful need to do the powerful thing better. If you insist on placing your freakin' nose in everyone's business then do it better!

EXACTLY, MR. REID

Senator Harry Reid was quoted this morning as saying "time to change the Senate before the institution becomes obsolete." Obviously, Mr. Reid didn't realize how confounding his statement sounds. Congress is already obsolete Harry. Perhaps Mr. Reid meant "officially" obsolete because if you Google the definition of obsolete even a crackhead knows this happened a long, long time ago with Congress. The close to single digit polling number that comes out every month is a result of polling the actual members of Congress. Take them out of the polling equation and the number becomes zero.

Mr. Reid, right know even your fellow democrats are laughing. Remember the old saying "Better to remain silent and be thought a fool than to speak and to remove all doubt." That's where you're at right now, buddy. Probably a good idea to just keep the pie hole shut. Maybe you and Joe Biden and Nancy Pelosi can go have a beer and laugh about all the dumb things you all say. Seriously, you guys are not helping your cause when you step up to the microphone.

You need to go to the congressional chalkboard (is there a congressional chalkboard?) and write out a hundred times "I will not speak before I think."

THE BILLS ARE PAID, TODAY

The bills, as of today, have been paid. That is what so many of us look forward to as a form of comfort. We sit back on the couch and breathe a sigh of relief that we made it through another month. We are the backbone of this nation because we are middle America or the beasts of burden as it seems some days. We know how lavishly the rich live and how disdainful those on the government dole are. The rich are able to be so because as consumers we buy what ever it is they produce and those on the dole, and I mean those who prefer to be on the dole, are taken care of by us, the taxpayer.

We complain to each other when we get together because we know the politicians aren't listening. We are anxious too often because we don't know how much we will have left over at the end of the month. Some look at us and see we may have a home or a nice car and our children are dressed well so our bank accounts must be flush with cash. But in order to have some semblance of the American Dream we need to spend money to have these things which we so rightly deserve. But after we pay the high cost of these items, because the rich feel their profit margins have to be high enough to support their lifestyles and the government takes most of the rest for those who don't want to work, it leaves little for us at the end of the month. And the media puts out daily something about government waste in the billions of dollars and CEO's and their executives get millions of dollars in bonuses as we pay nearly $4 a gallon at the pump. Celebrities and rock stars flaunt their wealth and then tell us how to think as if we are not capable ourselves. Who were these guys before they became celebrities and rock stars? I guess they forgot where they came from.

I would rather not hear that. I would prefer you just take my money and be done with it. I prefer not to hear about government waste that has always been and will always be. I don't want to hear about the record breaking quarter of any corporation and I would rather watch a movie or listen to some music without an actor or musician schooling me in life from the corridors of rehab.

Just shut up with all that stuff because this beast has a burden to carry.

HAS OBAMA MISSED AN OPPORTUNITY?

What greater platform exists than the Presidency of the United States? It commands the world's attention regardless of who holds the office. But a small number of men have been elected during a time of crisis and thus were given, if you will, the opportunity to accomplish feats that would forever change the world for the better. George Washington formed and shaped a new government that became the envy of the world. Lincoln healed a fractured nation and lead the charge resulting in the abolition of slavery. Franklin Delano Roosevelt brought the nation out of the Great Depression and led the nation through World War II. Harry Truman ended the Japanese aggression that gripped our nation. Kennedy averted a nuclear disaster. Reagan brought the United States back to its rightful place as the greatest nation on earth.

Each of these men were faced with a crisis when taking office or saw one develop during their watch. Each had an opportunity to be great and in this author's eyes they were. You can debate until the end of time which was the most effective in terms of what they accomplished in dealing with the crisis they were faced with. My money goes on Kennedy because it was quite possible there would no longer be an America if he hadn't stop the missiles from being fired that were sitting 50 miles off our coast.

President Obama, and this is not debatable due to the facts, assumed office during a time when the nation was involved in numerous wars and the closest thing to a Depression we have ever seen. This is what makes these men so special. Despite what he knew he was getting into, he still wanted it. Unlike Presidents who assumed office after their predecessor "fixed" everything, Obama was handed the worst situation possible. Whether you voted for him or not, once the newly elected President takes office, he is ours. There is only one President at a time for all of us. Like him or not, he's the guy. If your top quarterback goes down in a big game are you not going to support his backup? Of course you are because you still want to win the game. America wants to win regardless of who the quarterback is. If you could say there is an upside to his win, which really you can't because of what he inherited, you can say he was presented with a golden opportunity to bring the nation back to strength and greatness.

The question before us now is whether or not Barack Obama has taken advantage of this opportunity. Matters will not be fully and completely measured until scholars of history have their turn but for now we certainly have our opinions. Admittedly, things are better with the economy and the wars are winding down. Improvement in both these areas is the result of time and policy. The

President has no control over time but should have complete control over policy since he is our leader. There is only one leader in our form of democracy. Despite the leaders of the House and the Senate believing they are on par with the President, there is only one leader. So has the economy improved in the best way possible? Has the exit from the War on Terror been accomplished in the best way possible?

Do we need to wait for the scholars to provide these answers to us or are we savvy enough to at least proffer a somewhat intelligent answer now? And if the answer to both questions is no, can Obama turn them into yes before he leaves office? I think so which obviously gives away my position. I believe the President has stopped the bleeding but the pain still exists and more, and perhaps better, medical attention is required to get us back to full strength. That is easier said than done because of two undeniable facts and conditions that will never change. One is that a person who takes on something like the Presidency of the United States is without question an incredibly courageous person. Those of us who would never dream of doing this job cannot understand this courage but we know it exists. Most of us poop our pants when our checking account gets low. Secondly, there is the political system that seems to be designed to always be at odds and rightfully so because a nation based on a singular thought is called a dictatorship or Russia.

What I suspect has happened in the first instance is a courageous person became president but he hired people that are not so courageous to help him run things. In the second instance it is obvious to all mankind that the Congress has devolved into a brawl of sorts. I say of sorts because most of them are nerds and who has ever heard of nerds brawling?

Whether this will result in Obama being judged as harshly by historians as he is currently being judged by his critics, only time will tell. For the sake of argument let's say we didn't achieve the best possible results from the Administration's actions. Can a surgeon have a bad day? Sure (just as long as it's not my surgeon). Can we wheel the patient back into the operating room and make things better? Sure. Will President Obama's ego allow it? Therein lies the question of the moment. He should do what is right for all Americans. If it means admitting that maybe we should have done this differently or that differently, then admit it. If pulling out of Iraq and Afghanistan meant not doing anything for the Egyptians and Syrians it is not too late to adjust our thinking and our actions.

If repairing the economy meant we had to plunge the nation into an abyss of debt then it is not too late to adjust our thinking and our actions. Thus far nothing we have done is set in stone. Hell, we could even reverse Obamacare.

This president has an opportunity to go down in history as one of the greatest presidents ever. The choice is his. Even courageous people can make mistakes.

THE NEW GUY

The Taliban announced today they have elected a new leader since we whacked the last guy with a handy dandy drone strike. Don't you just love technology? To give you some idea of how nice of a guy this dirt bag is, he was the one who ordered the attack on the teenage girl activist who championed education for females. Now the world will have to keep the children indoors (but not in classrooms). After hearing the news I presume the United States government gassed up a new drone to send his way. If they didn't, they need to. What happened to the honor among thieves code? Assassinating children? Who is this guy?

We know who he is. He is a chair lift operator! In America we groom our commanders in schools like West Point and the Naval Academy. Over there they find them operating chair lifts. The guy went on to prominence because nothing was off limits to him. The more ruthless get the greatest amount of attention and then get promoted. Nothing is beyond this man. For all you bleeding hearts out there, study the man's history and even you will be calling for a drone strike!

So now we will spend countless man hours and endless dollars to track down this chair lift operator and kill him. And the only reason, and this dirt bag knows it, we will spend the hours and dollars is because everything we do is governed by partisan politics. It's not as simple as a conservative sitting in a room with a liberal and saying hey we need to go get this guy this afternoon. The liberal will most certainly respond by saying hold your horses big guy we need to deliberate about this for a couple of years and then, and only then, will we reluctantly agree. Just to make sure, the liberal will want more evidence of ruthlessness like a suicide bomb at a supermarket or some heads cut off or some bodies hanging from a bridge.

And then the liberal will wonder out loud if we actually have to kill him instead of capturing him and putting him on trial in Des Moine, Iowa but only after we read him his rights. There are two sides here. The good guys (us) and the bad guys (them). The bad guys don't bother with rules of engagement no matter how often that ineffectual body called the United Nations whines about it. On the other hand liberals spend countless hours creating new rules that they force on our military through the political process.

Even a liberal knows if he is lying on the ground as a victim of a robbery he will want to look up and see a cop.

POVERTY IS HERE TO STAY

So deal with it. Differently. What we are doing now is not working. It hasn't worked for a long time. According to the Federal Government in the year 2012 a family of four with an income of $23,238 or less fell into the poverty category. But our efforts to eliminate poverty have largely failed as evidenced by the phenomenal increase in the number of people now in that category.

The first thing you have to do is make poverty less attractive. There are plenty of legitimate studies out there that show that in the United States it is often more advantageous to some, if you want to live this way, to stay on the government dole rather than work full-time. Anyone on the government dole who has a shred of honesty in them would even admit it. If the difference of sitting on your couch or working full-time is negligible, it becomes a no-brainer to those who have no moral objections to living off the taxpayer.

Secondly, the populace that is usually in this category typically lack an educational history that would allow them to compete in a job market that is competitive and offers something better than a living wage. If a 30 year old man with a 9th grade education and married with two kids is limited to a fast food industry job alongside teenage students working part-time, he may see government assistance as attractive. Medical benefits, Section 8 housing, cash aid, and food stamps as an alternative can be enticing. What do you think encourages people from across the border to come here legally or illegally? So with those two dynamics at work a program to eliminate poverty is going to fall victim to an invitation to be cared for by the government.

Additionally, not all people desire to have a house in the suburbs and a BMW in the garage. If your standards or expectations are low than the offer of government assistance becomes attractive. So on the one hand you have the government wanting to eliminate poverty but on the other hand you have a population that prefers you leave well enough alone.

Therefore, poverty is here to stay!

PUT UP OR SHUT UP

I don't find that ObamaCare has a lot of attractive features but what I do see in it is an attempt to do something. All the naysayers spending every waking moment tearing it apart aren't coming up with an alternative. To say we didn't have to do anything with or to the system is like saying Iran isn't building a nuclear bomb. Duh. The naysayers want market forces to rule the day unfortunately that attitude comes from the 1% and the 1% wannabes. If the free enterprise system has devolved into a inequitable mess then something had to be done. In absence of a true partnership between the warring parties someone had to step up and it was the Democrats. Unfortunately, since Democrats love to coddle crackheads we ended up with what amounts to a national health care system designed for crackheads.

I am 61 years old and on a pension. No, not a 1% kind of pension but a working man's pension. I cannot afford $600 a month in health care especially if I see a doctor once or twice a year for something other than a heart transplant. But the naysayers don't give a crap about me, do they? Just ask Neil Cavuto. The fat cats want to peer down from their ivory towers and insist on the rest of us living the kind of life that they deem acceptable. If we don't live in that way we are parasites in their minds and are only after their money. Neil, I could give a flying f**k about what you say or do. I am a Fox News fan but will tune you out because I am tired of your disparaging remarks about middle America. I am happy you have made good in our great land of opportunity but I will thank you to stay the f**k out of my neighborhood. I know you would respond by saying you wouldn't be caught dead in my neighborhood which just adds weight to my assertion that you are a middle America hater.

I am an independent and I prefer to side with the conservatives but this time it is my wallet that dictates my thinking. The Republicans have no desire to tamper with the health care system which is obvious in their refusal to come up with a competing plan. Health care costs are out of freakin' control in the United States for the average citizen. They obviously aren't out of control to the wealthy because they have the deep pockets. Costs have to be dealt with in some way and the only one who stepped up was Obama. It is not by any stretch of the imagination a good plan but it is something at a time when something is needed badly.

So put up or shut up. If you can't or won't offer an alternative you just tell us you don't give a crap.

WHY I DON'T WANT MY SON TO JOIN THE MILITARY

Being a member of the military has always been a proud distinction. And although I am a strong supporter of the men and women who serve, I have asked my son not to join. His sister is a Marine and it was always his desire to do the same. I have a number of reasons for my feelings and I wish I didn't. In today's world it is not what it once was.

The President and many, if not most, in Congress have never served. You cannot fully understand how something works if your knowledge of it comes primarily from observation and late night pot smoking sessions. If you attended college, other than a military college, the textbooks only cover the military in a referential manner. And the political angle regarding the historical depiction of war is always a liberal one among college professors. Yet the individuals in power decide when and where we go to war. Once involved in war they decide how the military will prosecute the war. That's like the Amish telling you how to drive a truck. Just think about this for a moment. President Obama is the Commander-in-Chief. Go figure.

When you have a liberal, who has never served and would rather talk than fight, calling the shots for the military engaged in a war you have edicts like the one that requires that the enemy shoot first before we return fire. That never works in a war zone. What you really have is a police force provided by the United States and they are dressed in military uniforms. Our guys are soldiers not police officers.

And since we are in someone else's neighborhood we have to abide by their rules, laws, customs and freakin' weird ways of doing everything. Things that are part of everyday life there would be against the law in the States. It is known world-wide that Karzai and his co-horts are some of the most corrupt in the world. We made the guy a wealthy man by having to buy his favor. His term is about up so he is really talking s**t now since he knows the money spigot will be turned off when he leaves office. I realize we need military bulwarks in strategic locations but I won't believe we can't come up with better ways to do it. With all the brainiacs in charge you would think that we could come up with a better approach. And then the question that looms is whether the strategic placement of our troops is for the purpose of protecting the personal safety of the American people.

The government always tells us it is to protect our "national interests." Well, our safety is definitely a national interest but so is our business interests in the region and that is where things get murky. Even though we get enough oil out of our own ground, the oil that comes out of their ground is sold to us at a much cheaper rate. Think about it, the United States sells its own oil to other countries and we turn around and buy oil from countries in which we are conducting war and from countries that truly hate us, like Venezuela. This is part of a formula the oil companies use which makes them record profits but is rarely translated into lower prices at America's gas pumps. So you have to ask yourself if the troops are being used for the benefit of the politicians and the oil companies wouldn't that make our troops a private security force for those interests? And if you don't understand the correlation of the government and the oil companies then you're an idiot and should be reading the funny papers instead of this article.

Every time a people in another part of the world live in a way contrary to the American way, we want to go over and start killing people. The war hawks in Congress never change and seemingly never go away. America is a country not a world. The world is made up of countries that choose to live the way they live and no matter how disgusting we find it, it is not our job to fix it. An exception to that would be if a tyrant were to wreak horrific carnage on his own people then there would be the question of whether or not we should step in to stop the bloodshed. Well, we see that all the time the most recent case being Syria. Syria proves we don't step in to stop the bloodshed. Instead, we talk about it with other world leaders and pontificate while doing nothing. Of course the war hawks would just bomb the entire country and be done with it. But John McCain never gets his way these days. And apparently Syria is not vital to our business interests.

Let's touch on the subject of winning wars. We don't. We fight wars but we don't win wars. Vietnam is communist. We have been embroiled in war in the Middle East for more than a dozen years. We have won nothing. Even in the countries in the region where we are currently fighting to set up a democratic form of government, it rarely resembles what we have. In fact, it is so unlike our democratic form of government any passerby would have to be told that what they are seeing is the formation of somebody's idea of a democratic government just not ours. How about the democratic form of government they set up in Egypt? How's that working for them?

Now for the coup de grace. As I stated earlier our son's sister is a Marine and we have not agreed with how she has been treated. We can't say anything to her because she is a proud Marine. Just the way the Marines like them. Much easier to manipulate. We do not want our son subjected to that. I personally am a proud American who supports our troops 1000% but that does not mean I agree with the brass. If we are attacked by another then I would not be averse to using the same tactics the enemy uses and the larger the bombs we drop the better. But that is not how it works. These wars are decided by panty waste politicians most of whom have not served and couldn't beat their way out of a wet paper bag. And they want to send our children to fight for them. I don't want my kids fighting for them, I want my kids fighting for America. America is not socialist Obama, wimpy Harry Reid, cry baby John Boehner, war hawk John McCain, or any number of these idiots running the country like they are Keystone Cops.

The latest atrocity is the handling of the case of Reserve Maj. Jason Brezler. Jason Brezler is a decorated Marine, a New York firefighter, and a good man. If we had good men in Congress the poll ratings of Congress wouldn't be near a single digit. If you don't know the case then Google it and enlighten yourselves. That being said, the crux of the case is that Mr. Brezler exposed an Afghan official on the payroll of the United States who has abetted the enemy, trafficked in narcotics and arms, and has been accused of sexual assaults on numerous children while on a U.S. base. Damn. How do you react to that? The way you react to that is by doing what Jason Brezler did yet because of a technicality he is being thrown out of the Marines and the Afghan thug rides another day. Talk about the brass not having the soldier's back. The Marines never leave one of their own behind, right? Apparently that is not the case with upper management. I have a sneaking suspicion, only because this stuff happens almost daily, that Hamid Karzai went to our guys and said if you want more out of me you better back off my Afghan buddy. He's protecting his own. Something we might consider doing. Again, if you jump on the Net and research how child molestation occurs and is handled in Afghanistan, you are going to vomit. And for this stuff to happen on a U.S. base then some heads of brass should be rolling not the head of Jason Brezler.

Our brave men and women who serve as soldiers are being victimized by politicians and high ranking military leadership. They are being underpaid, worked too hard, and not given nearly as many benefits as they should when leaving the military especially the wounded. Yet when told to go to war, even if it is a war we shouldn't be in, they follow orders and give their lives. Our daughter had nothing but good intentions upon joining and she remains a dedicated warrior. It was her choice to join. We tried but couldn't stop her.

So here we are again. This time I hope we succeed. Politicians who get us into unjust wars and military leadership that leaves behind a warrior like Jason Brezler, don't deserve another of our children.

UNAUTHORIZED AIDES

Why do we always hear from "unauthorized aides" if they are unauthorized. I scoured every source known to mankind to understand this because I thought it was just me. I thought maybe I didn't understand the word unauthorized. Anyway, now I do. It is, in fact, Washington Speak. It means that they put the dumb-ass aide out there to say what the boss won't say and when the s**t hits the fan, another aide (an authorized one) claims he was not authorized to comment therefore don't pay any attention to what the unauthorized aide said.

This behavior is one that has been around forever and we all do it. We do it when we want to go into the water. We creep up to the water's edge and stick the tips of our toes in to see how cold it is. Suffice it to say, the aide is the tips of the toes of the boss! As far as I am concerned I could not be in a job wherein I am treated like the tips of someone's toes. But for those who aspire to rise in the ranks of thugs, I mean politicians, abject humiliation is required. Since politicians pretty much give up their souls for what they do then it is no big deal. It's all in a day's work.

And lest they think we don't know, whenever the unauthorized aide speaks we know something really bad has happened. When it is no big deal a politician will step up and say “my bad' and make it appear he took the high road and he is actually a human being. But when the s**t is about to hit the fan the office Chief of Staff will go down the flunky list to see who is next up and push that guy to the podium with a scripted response. The next day they trot out the selected “authorized aide” to debunk whatever the unauthorized aide said because now the politician who f**ked up has had time to come up with an excuse he thinks people will buy.

The above was written by me not an unauthorized aide.

IN A NUTSHELL

Health and Human Services Secretary Kathleen Sebelius's remark today in response to a Republican push to have her resign is the ultimate illustration of the way politicians think. Her remark was that she didn't work for those who are calling for her resignation. It makes no difference that she works for a president that is an avowed Democrat; it would be the same if the President was a Republican. She made the remark to a media that usually provides protection to the Democratic Party. Or maybe they missed it?

It is probably safe to assume the Republicans calling for her resignation are taxpayers. And since they are taxpayers, Ms. Sebelius, you do work for them. As a matter of fact I too am calling for your resignation. Maybe you didn't hear me because I am on the West Coast. I yelled as loud as I could but apparently you weren't listening. I am a registered Independent that pays taxes. Do you work for me?

Politicians of every ilk need to think before they speak. Highly educated people who have achieved a significant amount of success in their lives and are charged with the responsibility of representing citizens, need to think before they speak. The good thing about that is you will cut down considerably the amount of dumb stuff that comes out of your mouths. I mean really people. Show some restraint. We deserve it.

Secretary Sebelius's behavior is not unusual except that it was on full display for millions to view on the television. Her arrogance is pervasive among those who do Washington's work. If a president is elected he works for all the people and in turn the people he brings on board work for all the people.

So yes, Secretary Sebelius, you do work for those who are calling for your resignation.

UP CLOSE AND PERSONAL

It wasn't that I didn't pay attention to my medical care costs it's just that I have always had a Cadillac policy so my out of pocket expenses were minimal. I have always known, as has everyone with half a brain, that medical costs were outrageous. You see stories about it all the time. But I never saw it up close until the other day. I got a prescription for Ibuprofen with Famotidine. My doctor said the inclusion of Famotidine with the Ibuprofen was to prevent or minimize any stomach problems. Anyway, when I got home and looked at the personal prescription information that came with it, it had a notation by the pharmacy that the retail price was $680.29 for 90 tablets. Even though I was sitting reclined in my recliner, I fell out of it! Are you freakin' kidding me? That's about $7.56 a tablet. This is for Ibuprofen. You can buy Ibuprofen over the counter. Hell, you can buy it at the 99 cent store. Maybe the inclusion of the Famotidine is what put it over the top. Maybe Famotidine is a miracle drug and I didn't know it.

If Famotidine is some kind of super expensive compound because you have to drill to the center of the earth or go to the moon to mine it, I could maybe understand why it is so expensive. But I think not. I think what I saw up close and personal is exactly why people like President Obama is hell bent on a national health plan. It's because we are getting stroked by the health care industry. The big players in the industry are getting rich by stroking the common man.

Now we all know, mostly from the oil industry, that if we complain about outrageous pricing they don't give a crap! I was going to say it falls on deaf ears but I didn't because we know they hear us which means they don't give a crap. I'm definitely not a liberal and I certainly am not a Democrat. I prefer the status of Independent. But I put this squarely on the shoulders of the conservatives. They are unwilling to consider health care reform. The Health Care Lobby is well funded and very persuasive. Their responsibility is clear, protect the status quo. With the unprecedented attempt to finally upend the industry the White House has certainly provoked both negative and positive responses. The Health Care Lobby has partnered with the only ones in Congress they can count on, the Republicans.

The effort by the Republicans to kill the Affordable Care Act failed. But that isn't stopping them. They hope to gain enough Republican support with the mid-term elections and the Oval Office in 2016 and with that support, overturn the law.

Good luck with that one.

HOW BEING STUPID IS REALLY NOT A GOOD IDEA

The kind of stupid I am talking about is the kind of stupid a person chooses. I am not actually talking about the developmentally challenged so all of you crusaders of political correctness need not get your shorts in a bunch. I am talking about the person, despite all the educational opportunities available, who decides thanks but no thanks. The gang life is fine with me or I don't mind the government taking care of me or any number of bull s**t reasons you may come up with. In any case I don't think it is really a good idea to maintain elective stupidity. Whatever life stupidity gets you it is no way near what you could have if you became unstupid (that's not a real word).

Let's look at the gang life. In the gang life it is always a small percentage at the top, the gang 1% if you will, that make all the money. And what typically happens to them? They die by gunfire or spend life in prison. When was the last time you went to a retirement party, unless you want to call a funeral one, of a drug 1%'er? And to be honest the leaders are not actually stupid they are just too lazy to manage their intellect by going to school or something. In other words, they want the easy money. They want easy money, fast women (even slow women), fancy cars and cool houses. They want to stay up all night partying and doing their drugs. And they are willing to accept the consequences.

Now lets look at the professional welfare recipient. I don't have any problem with a welfare system that helps out those who need help while getting back on their feet. I have a problem with the person who decides on a being a welfare recipient as a career. And in America, thanks to democrats, you can do that. And the system is designed to specifically aid the stupid.

They have dumbed down the process so that if your a slobbering idiot it will be a breeze. In fact, if you show up and you can put together a coherent sentence it will cause suspicion. These kinds of people lack a moral or ethical compass so they do not question what they do but instead keep in front of them at all times their mission which is to secure money from the government, it is legal and easy. In too many instances it has devolved into a generational behavior. Each succeeding generation is schooled in the art of gaining access to the government coffers. There is no attempt to break the cycle because in their minds the cycle is productive. Cash, food, housing and medical care is what the cycle produces. These people refuse to be shamed into change and the government almost invites them to take part in the system.

Unfortunately, no part of this system of gifting requires,

provides, or even encourages education therefore the stupidity continues.

WHAT'S WRONG WITH SOLITARY CONFINEMENT?

Let's be honest here. Or at least I will be honest here. The people I am going to talk about are not honest. Not honest with themselves so it would be likely they are not honest with anyone. People who are of an extreme liberal persuasion, and I do say that with prejudice because I am being honest, are all wrong on the issue of solitary confinement in American prisons. I did work in a jail for many years so I do not come to this opinion unarmed. The people who are protesting the conditions of solitary confinement are not conservative. They are all liberal because it is a liberal cause. And it is, for the most part, the same group that wants to abolish the death penalty. In fact the argument I am making should actually begin with the death penalty issue. You know the old saying that s**t flows downhill? That's why we have to start with the death penalty.

The liberals promoting the abolition of the death penalty are using a tried and proven method to reach their goal. It is a method found in all efforts when it comes to a significant change in the way America does business. It is to portray an America that is uncivil in their approach to the incarceration of their citizens. And the only way to return to civility is to make major changes to the system in favor of the incarcerated.

But let's look at this in a practical way. Does our penal system really need change? Of course it does. You can't operate a system the size of our penal system without having a bunch of problems. But when we talk about the death penalty or the use of solitary confinement we are talking about the top tier of criminals. Criminals who murder, rape, molest, kidnap, and deal drugs to our children. Criminals which studies (many studies over a long period of time) show they will commit these crimes again. A murderer commits murders, even in prison. A sexual pervert commits sex acts, even in prison. A doper does drugs, even in prison. So if you have these guys in the general population all these things will happen which will result in them being removed to special units or solitary confinement. There is existing evidence to prove my point. If a criminal is in prison for committing a crime and while in prison commits a crime, what is wrong with solitary confinement? He obviously isn't getting it.

And regarding the death penalty, if a lawyer is successful in getting a prisoner's death penalty verdict overturned, where do you put them? In the general population? Wouldn't that be nice for the prisoner. If the death penalty is converted to life in prison then there is the possibility of parole because there is really no such thing as life without parole. That is a device used to pacify the citizenry who want the judicial system to work. So it is quite possible that a murderer who was once sentenced to death could eventually walk the streets again only to kill again. Does that make sense to anyone?

I can accept a moratorium on the death penalty only because we have numerous prisoners on death row dating from a time when law enforcement did not have the advantage of DNA evidence. I'm sure many of us are aware of recent cases being overturned based on new DNA evidence in which they found the convicted to be innocent. There is a long history of overzealous prosecutors who cared more about their conviction rate then the guilt of the defendant. In those days we didn't have the advantage of DNA testing to keep these idiots from ruining the lives of innocent people.

Once we rehabilitate the death penalty process I have no problem with the reinstatement of it in certain, extreme cases. And solitary confinement is a tool needed by prison staff to maintain control and should remain in place.

IT'S REALLY NOT THAT DIFFICULT

Listen up boys and girls! I have had it up to my eyeballs with this crap in Washington. The s**t they have to deal with ain't that difficult. I don't care how much money they have or how highly educated they are, the s**t is not that difficult. Foreign policy , domestic policy, and any other policy is only as difficult as they make it. And I believe they try to make it difficult on purpose to keep Middle America in the mind set of needing them because they think it is beyond our intellectual reach.

And I also believe they do this because of their relationship with special interests. Think about it. If you were to deal with each of these issues on their merits alone it would be pretty cut and dry. Foreign aid would go to countries that had a legitimate need and had, or were willing to accept, a plan to deal with whatever their crisis happens to be. But when you factor in American business interests and national security issues then foreign aid is determined more on how much we need them than a particular country's needs. Our needs may include a way to quickly strike militarily at those in the region who would want to hurt us but it might be business interests because a company can make more for their investors over there than here.

So does that make the U.S. government a flunkey for

Corporate America? That's a tough one to argue because it sure appears so. So the next logical question would be "Does the U.S. military presence over there protect us or America's business interests?" Do corporate interests enjoy the use of a private security force paid for by American taxpayers?

Perhaps what is so difficult in conducting foreign policy is how much work has to go into concealing its true intent.

FIX YOUR COUNTRIES!

In the wake of the horrific deaths of migrants in the Mediterranean Sea political leaders in the region sprang into action with the requisite platitudes. Their cries for help are hollow and meant more as a gesture expected of a leader. Leaders are not defined by what they say but what they do. There are countries all across the globe led by men who who talk like leaders but loot like bandits. And a common thread running through all these leaders is that whatever happens that is bad is the fault of someone else and whatever happens that is good is because of something they did.

While it is a tragedy that so many lives are lost because they simply want to go somewhere so they can have a life, it doesn't fix the core problem. And meaningless language from leaders won't fix it either. The important question that is never raised because it means having to react is why people feel forced to leave the country they were born in and love? I know they love their country because immigrants everywhere, legal or not, often express the love for their former home even while living in the home of another. So it begs the question why don't they fix their country? They can use as a model whatever country they desire to migrate to. For instance, if a Mexican citizen wants to migrate to America and will risk their life to do so, wouldn't it be a better idea to change your country so that it resembles America more? If you are willing to risk your life crossing a barren Arizona desert, why wouldn't you be willing to risk your life to change your own country? America is the way it is because a rag tag group of colonists risked their lives to make it so.

In almost every instance it is a relatively small group that exerts the stranglehold on a country. Whether it be radical Islamists, dictators, Cartels, Elitists, or Vladimir Putin, it is small albeit powerful. Once the power is wrested from them you have a country primed for change. We saw it recently with the Arab Spring. The problem there is they took the power from one despot and gave it to another. Seriously people, you might want to put a little bit more thought into it before you lay down your life.

It has been shown time and again that the only form of government that doesn't have its people fleeing the country is the democratic model. Granted, we do have our problems but I will take our problems over your problems any day of the week! If you don't like the America version of democracy, create your own. Apply it to your own country and develop something you don't want to leave and future generations will continue to build on.

IT JUST BOGGLES THE MIND

I read today that British scientists were able to stop the death of brain cells in mice. This has far reaching implications for the treatment of Alzheimer's and Parkinson's disease. The study was definitive. They were able to stop the disease in all the effected subjects. But, they went on to say it could be 10 years before human trials begin. WTF? Are you kidding me? Why in the world would something this important have to take 10 years before we even “start” human trials? I can only surmise that it has something to do with Special Interests. I use that term with caps because they are a specific group that impacts our daily lives in every way. And not in a small way but a major way. And let me say that it is my opinion that these Special Interests do not give a s**t what we think or feel. They only care about the amount of money they can generate. Now you can bend that to say it indirectly helps everyone eventually but must go through the Special Interests process. In most cases I imagine it is territorial among them in terms of the competition in our free market system. I understand that but in some areas we have to make exceptions to the rule and get an item to market STAT. Some things are just too important to not put the full weight of the government and the private sector behind it. In the case of making people whole again there should be no doubt as to the importance of expediency. If a condition such as Alzheimer’s is costing the taxpayers millions but doesn't appeal to Corporate America as something that would generate gargantuan profits then perhaps the government should step up and convince the company that in the long run it would be in their best interests to get a cure to market post haste. Unfortunately, Washington has decided to be the lap dog of Corporate America which leaves it impotent.

We can cure Alzheimer's. If we can produce all the advances the world has witnessed over the last 50 years then we can cure Alzheimer's. It all comes down to money. We have seen for the longest time millionaires and even billionaires created almost overnight mostly through technology breakthroughs or something having to do with social media. It seems what gets invented is that which makes the quickest and most money.

If we have the talent and the money then the only thing lacking is a desire. A desire to make the world right for Alzheimer's sufferers and their families. The only way we are going to get the desire is to learn to prioritize in a way that places people before money.

TRY TO KEEP YOUR EYE ON THE BALL

It happens all the time, unfortunately. People, or in this case groups, will not keep their eye on the ball because they look at America with tunnel vision. All they can focus on is their own particular problem and nothing is going to keep them from doing that. It matters not what the emergent issue is at the moment, their issue always trumps it. So even though it would benefit all of us if we could all come together to tackle a pressing problem, it ain't gonna happen. Groups get, and it is their decision, so fixated on their issue they won't think that by taking a break from their issue they could actually resolve another issue; one that impacts us all.

Well, let me tell you something boys and girls. When you do this it really backfires on you in the end. I believe I speak for a lot of people when I say we get pretty pissed off at the selfishness of groups keeping their issue center stage as if life depended on it. The next time they look for my support I'm going to remember we didn't get their support. Anywhere from the organized labor movement to small fringe groups we see this single issue phenomenon and every group wants their cause to be the one everyone focuses on.

So the focus actually becomes so fragmented that not one issue gets sufficient attention so as to make a difference.

This causes the supporters of one particular issue to double down which takes any attention they might have expended on a more universal issue, away. The result is nothing gets accomplished and the issue is allowed to worsen or, in the least, remain the same.

Issues don't resolve themselves.

MUCH ADO ABOUT NOTHING

With the full realization that it is an epic change to the national landscape, I still have to wonder about all the political consternation surrounding this event. I mean, we all knew it was coming someday. Hillary tried to warm us to the idea during her time as the First Lady. And as soon as she had her own eye on the Presidency we knew it would come roaring back. The times dictate it as well. It's not like this isn't happening anywhere else. The United States is actually lagging behind among industrialized nations when it comes to healthcare. We didn't even have the bandwagon in sight until Hillary forced the conversation on us.

Of course, as always, Middle America of both political persuasions has to take a back seat to special interests. I say both political persuasions because conservatives have tried to drop this squarely in the lap of liberal America. I'm of a conservative mind and I want national healthcare. So there. I am not alone in my thinking lest you try to separate me from the pack and call me an anomaly. I am a political independent who happens to think more conservatively. I am 61 years old and forced to retire early. I will not be eligible for Medicare until I turn 65. That means I have to pay upwards of five hundred dollars a month for medical benefits. Since I am Middle America

I do not have a gargantuan pension coming in every

month so budgeting is the order of the day.

Also at my age I have been around several blocks and paid enough attention to know that the oil and insurance industries dominate our day to day lives more than we are willing to admit. Special interests aside, if the argument is one of financial feasibility, since it is a tax supported program, is it the Middle America taxpayer complaining or is it the conservative party claiming to represent us? Since I am never asked by a conservative, or a liberal for that matter, what my opinion is then I believe it is not the taxpayer complaining. If they want to trot out a pollster that claims polls show one thing or another then they have to do better than asking 3 people in the break room what they think. If Middle America has accepted millions of people on the welfare rolls and disability payments to crackheads than why would they object to getting help for themselves?

What it comes down to is Washington's approach to the national budget. The guys on both sides of the aisle care only about the numbers and how that may effect their chances of re-election. They don't see us. I know this because if they did they would show up in our lives somewhere other than the 5:00 o'clock news. It has been common knowledge since the beginning of mankind that politicians cannot handle money. I mean, our money.

They do very well handling their own money. If they aren't rich when they enter politics they are usually rich when they leave. By the way, how does that happen? That's a story for another time.

Back to the cost of The Affordable Care Act because that's what it is really about. I say that because I don't want to believe my representatives in Washington don't want me to have healthcare. It is actually simple and easy to fund The Affordable Care Act. I am not a number cruncher so bear with me. I even forget the number of beers I drink during a football game although I am reminded the next morning.

Anyway, all it takes is a few minutes of tweaking the budget to get the money to assure all Americans have proper healthcare. Which is actually a noble cause. It is an action that could make politicians legitimately proud. We can start with government waste. If we even slightly reduce government waste we could fund the program until the end of time. Just the amount Hamid Karzai pocketed would do the job. And if we stop building bridges to nowhere we would have money left over. Imagine that. The liberals could give the crackheads a raise! But I am just getting started. How about we take a break from war? Think about the money we could save there not to mention the lives of our sons and daughters. Remember, I am conservative but I certainly wouldn't prosecute a war the way we do. I would leave the special interests at home until we got the job done. They seem to f**k everything up.

It is shameful that the greatest country on earth has their citizens paying astronomical sums of money for health care and that is if they can afford it. The Affordable Care act is far from perfect with its biggest flaw being that if you don't buy insurance you will be penalized. That smacks of socialism. But the fact is we needed something, especially in the senior community where we have just enough money to get by although not enough to buy individual health insurance. We make too much to qualify for medi-cal which puts us in financial limbo.

And since we give untold amounts of money to support foreign countries and America's crackheads what is the big deal about some affordable health insurance?

CONGRESS NEEDS A TIME-OUT

When children misbehave they get a time-out. When Congress misbehaves they too should get a time-out. After all, they are acting like children. And what's up with that anyway? Aren't these guys like really smart? If that's the case why is it so damn hard for them to do their job? Or maybe, just maybe being a legislator isn't that hard. If that's true then sign me up. I would love all those perks! What job can you have, other than being a rock star, where you can get pampered the way Congress is pampered? Let's just say these guys are actually smart. We know you don't have to use that intelligence to get elected because all politicians say the same thing and it is the same thing politicians have been saying since the beginning of mankind. It' all platitudes with some handshaking and baby kissing stuff as the camera is rolling. If the economy is bad they say they will fix it. They don't say how, they just say they will fix it. If we are in a war they say we will get out or we will bomb even more. It depends on what party is talking. If crime is a problem both parties will hire more cops.

My point here is that once they get to Congress we hope they will draw from that intellectual bank and come up with solutions. So after the debilitating chaos of the election process we can look forward to the new session of Congress. Right? Unfortunately, something happens when that session starts. I don't know if they are administered stupid pills but I wouldn't be surprised. And it doesn't matter what their political persuasion is because it happens across the board. Both sides of the aisle suddenly become stupid! And they don't even try to hide it. They put it right out there. They do it at press conferences for the entire world to see. They have absolutely no shame. If in Middle America, meaning those of us not under the influence of crack, is turning to each other and remarking what the f**k just happened, we are in big trouble. If you are asking each other if the legislator at the podium actually said what you think he said, we are in big trouble.

Now there is a reason why these guys poll so low. It's not the way they dress because we pay them enough to buy the finest threads. It is not the way they speak because they all speak eloquently. It's that what they speak so eloquently they don't do. Hello? Americans know what bull s**t is no matter how eloquently you present it. We need and deserve action. And action that results in improved lives for Americans. You keep taking our money and mismanaging it when it should be used to improve our standard of living.

We need to change our system that would allow the citizens to remove from office any representative that is performing poorly. We do this in the private sector and it somehow motivates workers to do better.

FREEDOM

If you ask someone, particularly in America, how they would define freedom you would get a standard, sanitized version that somewhat resembles what we were raised to believe. In reality, we have numerous versions of the original concept and they are fluid. Activists on both sides of the issue are adamant in their beliefs yet as they argue those beliefs, freedom is changing right in front of their own eyes. One side claims the tenets of freedom are cast in stone with Constitutional protection. Others feel it was always meant to be a concept that would change with time and societal norms. Although I am more inclined to agree with the former I am observant enough to realize it is the latter who is winning. The concept we know as freedom is changing daily at the behest of politicians, special interests, religion, and lawyers. Power and money is what shapes our idea of freedom today. And those of us who reside in Middle America can do nothing about it. It is a force far greater than any force we could cobble together. We see on the daily news how small extremists groups can control parts of the world without fear they will be stopped. If that can happen what do you think the most powerful nation in the world can do?

What freedom has done to us is allowed us to be a selfish people. I am not referring to the kind of selfishness we typically experience within our homes with our children and our spouses. I am referring to the selfishness of groups which take the act of selfishness to levels far beyond the comprehension of the ordinary person. The kind of person that resides in Middle America.

Middle America is a place you find most of us. It is metaphysical, not geographical. It is where you find the middle income, law-abiding, family oriented, tax paying people who are the backbone of this country. Without us you don't have a country. When America needs money, we provide it. When America needs protection from our enemies, we provide it. When America needs safe passage walking her streets, we provide it. We provide it by allowing money to be taken from our weekly paychecks. We provide it because our children volunteer to be soldiers, peace officers and fireman. And after that what do we get? We get politicians who could not care less about what we think or they would ask us. We get wealthy people who sit in their 10,000 square feet homes complaining we take too much of their earnings so therefore we are parasites. In our churches it is their way or the highway. And if you don't travel down their highway you will surely end up in Hell. If it is a Muslim world you will die a horrible death in a shopping mall.

And if things don't go the way of the politician they simply make a call to the Supreme Court and take care of the matter once and for all. Understand though, if the call comes from someone in Middle America the phone will not be answered.

In fact, you have to own a special phone when you make that call.

WE TRIED, IT DIDN'T WORK, LET'S GET OUT

We need to pull out now! Totally and completely. Leave no advisers, soldiers, contractors, equipment, or money. We have already given them too much. They don't deserve any more. I am talking about Afghanistan but I believe we should do the same thing in the entire region. I don't even want to have a diplomatic presence there. You can bring up all the reasons we have used over all the years and they mean nothing! These people are not going to change. They are certainly not going to change in the way we hope they would. We have nothing to gain from them. There are plenty of countries we can get our oil from because when it comes right down to it, it's about the oil. I don't want to get into a discussion about oil right now because it never ends well. It's the proverbial 800 pound gorilla.

The reasons for being there are no longer valid. We have lost too many lives and have spent too much money. Money we didn't even have. My grandchildren will be paying payments on money loaned to us by China that went in Hamid Karzai's pocket. Does this make any sense to you? We obviously didn't learn from Vietnam. It seems

Washington doesn't understand when things are going poorly you either fix it or get the hell out. Everyone knows we haven't been able to fix anything in that region. In many ways things are worse. So get out. We survived what many considered a loss in Vietnam and we will survive this. And who gives a crap what anyone says about the United States? If they are talking smack they aren't our friends and our friends are smart enough to know they should remain our friends. So really what is the downside of getting the f**k out of there?

If it is the loss of oil revenues then say it. Be honest and say "We are there for the corporations and not the average Joe in America." We can handle that. We've handled a lot of political crap over the years. We are a resilient bunch. We know we will never get a political system that actually works so we will take the flawed version as long as you don't destroy democracy (see Obama and Socialism).

The bottom line is we can't spend any more American lives on an effort that has failed. Time for Plan B.

IT'S NOT ABOUT THE EVIDENCE

It's not about the evidence. The evidence was always there in some form. It doesn't take much evidence to convince people who just watched a dictator oversee the death of over 100,000 of his citizens. First, it is about Americans, and much of the rest of the "civilized" world, who are tired of war. It has gone on for too long already and it needs to stop. Secondly, it is about how ineffective a strike of any kind would be. Even those of us who are couch potatoes enjoying a good Jerry Springer show know that a strike of the kind being discussed is not going to work. The whack jobs running these countries are hell bent on disrupting the balance in this world and they don't scare that easy anymore. Thirdly, they have that short little ego tripper running Russia barking about protecting Syria and its murderous regime. Who knows what this guy will do? He hates most everybody except for his entourage of sycophants. And lastly, and that's not to say these are the only valid points, it is about the money. America's got problems. Better looking stock market numbers, a spike in housing, or a improved employment rate hardly means we have emerged from the Great Recession. We would spend millions upon millions to fire Tomahawk missiles for three days into an area that is probably now a vacant lot because Assad has had time to re-locate everything we would hope to destroy. What ever happened to the element of surprise? And then three days after that we would provide an aid package of billions (which we will find two years from now that half of it can't be accounted for) to rebuild and most of that money would buy weapons to kill Americans.

Mr. President, we voted for you to fix our country and in doing so get us out of the war zone. Don't go all John McCain on us. Find another way to get the chemical weapons out of Assad's control and let the Syrian people handle their own affairs. Time, and the death of too many American soldiers, have done nothing to improve the situation in that part of the world. You are tall and Vladimir Putin is short. Studies have shown that tall people are more likely to succeed. So bark back when that junkyard dog barks and he will scamper off. And if you are doing this for political reasons then...well, I'm not going to disparage the office of the President but needless to say that would be bull s**t.

I feel horrible about what happened to those innocent civilians in Syria but we can't get involved in every problem that occurs in the world. Since the beginning of mankind the earth has been populated with psychopathic people who have no feelings when it comes to killing innocent people. History 101 explains that. If we had an effective United Nations they could create and deploy a multi-national special forces team to assassinate these whack job killing machines and the world would remain in balance. Now for those who believe that is a horrific idea, you must think gassing people, torture, and prison camps are okay. Cut off the head of the snake and you will have a better chance of controlling a situation. We already know this because to some extent we apply that philosophy now.

The gassing of Syrian civilians is a symptom, albeit a terrible one, of a much greater problem. By dropping bombs a month after the event it is like scolding a child for something he did a few days ago. It won't be understood. I know that example can be viewed as making light of the situation but it is an accurate example nonetheless. The rest of the world, including the Muslim population, has already accepted the gas attack evidenced by their lack of support for retaliation.

As the most powerful nation in the world (are you listening Vladimir) we are tasked with the top leadership position. But even the greatest leaders don't get their way sometimes. Let's fight the battles we can win and let's fight them our way. As I always say, we are the biggest and the baddest and we need to stop trying to please everyone else. The world knows we strive to do the right thing usually when many of them are doing the wrong thing.

OUT THE FRONT DOOR, IN THE BACK DOOR

I cannot believe how gullible we are. Vladimir Putin is being hailed as the one leader who was able to come up with a diplomatic solution to avert a military strike on Syria while our leader talked the thing to death and all the other leaders sat on their hands. Listen up people, spend a few minutes on the internet to school yourself. Where do you think Syria gets their weapons? Hello! They get them from Russia. Now Russia has never denied their relationship with Syria and the fact they are Syria's main weapons supplier. What they are not admitting, despite Secretary of Defense Chuck Hagel's assertion, is that they supplied Syria with chemical weapons. Okay folks, lets do the math. Do you really think Russia said no way when Syria was looking for help in creating a chemical weapons program? They know that if they don't help Syria, Syria will go to another country which will diminish the relationship between the two. Syria is the only strategic location where Russia can park their ships in the Middle East even though they are surrounded by numerous and strategically placed American military bulwarks. It's still better than having no presence at all for the country that has, since WWII, been battling the United States for control of the region. We also know that these Middle Eastern nations have perfected the act of pimping the United States so why wouldn't they pimp Russia?

So this is what is going to happen, in my opinion. Russia will broker this deal between the United States, Syria, and the United Nations. Russia will get their 15 minutes of fame (unless Putin puts his foot in his mouth again and that 15 minutes is cut down to 10) and the United States will spend another exhaustive week talking about our credibility. After the chemical weapons go out the front door of Syria and are dumped in the hazard waste bin, in the back door will come a fresh supply. In other words, Syria will launder weapons the same way Cartels launder money.

The world is stroking us. We are like the little kid on the playground being bullied for his money. But we respond with such eloquent language to this debacle that people don't realize it is a debacle. We "sound" powerful but are we? When was the last time we won a war? When was the last time we admitted to losing billions of dollars in Afghanistan or Iraq. I'm not talking about the money that is actually spent on infrastructure that will never be appreciated or used to its full capacity.

I'm talking about the billions that have disappeared and we will never know where it went. Even a dumb-ass will realize it will go to buy weapons of the chemical type. These countries take our tax dollars and spread them around so the rogue nations will get American dollars that were never meant for them. Hell, we can't even keep track of the money in our own country. How could we ever keep track of our money in those thug nations. Do you think Hamid Karzai is living large? I rest my case.

The sad thing about all of this is we continually talk about our credibility around the world and these guys are laughing out loud at us. They don't really hate us. That would be like a druggie hating his dealer. They don't hate us. They know they can bite the hand that feeds and every time they talk s**t about us we give them more money to shut them up. They are working us and we call it "diplomacy."

So now Russia has jumped on the pimping bandwagon. Putin is taking a break from suppressing his own people to join Syria in this international game. You know he is just trying to distract people from focusing on how he is screwing his own citizens. And you talk about credibility. Putin does the stuff he does to his own people, which is well documented, and then he gains instant credibility by brokering the Syria deal. That should tell you how bogus this credibility thing is.

So our guy goes on television in an expensive suit with American regalia in the background and with eloquent speech (I gotta give Obama props for that) and reassures the world that everything will be alright because we have dismantled the latest crisis with the help of a tyrant.

So much for credibility.

WHY THE BEST AND THE BRIGHTEST GET NO RESPECT

It's a sad time in America. It is for me anyway. And I suspect there are many, too many, others out there who feel this same sadness. It is a sadness that has evolved from an anger that was never addressed. Those of us who are not psychopathic, or have not been revealed as such, have been feeling the complete range of emotions over a long period of time that has devolved into a profound sadness. A sadness that reveals surrender as being the only option. A sadness that our legislators in this great country have failed miserably.

We have all felt that sadness at certain points in our lives most of us when we were teenagers feeling that no matter what we said or did it changed nothing. We would talk to adults who simply would not listen. They were convinced that they knew what was best for us and nothing we said could change that. It is sort of how I feel now. We vote, we write, we email, we protest in the street yet it falls on deaf ears. Personally, I have never felt so helpless. Legislators today, and I don't have to offer evidence because unless you live under a rock in Lower Slobovia (I apologize to Slobovians), it hits you in the face every single day. And what makes it so much worse is they don't give a s**t. They won't even acknowledge it despite the polls and the scandals and the worldwide revelations splashed all over the social media. They don't even throw us a bone. And lest you try to read this as political it involves all political parties. Politicians have become so arrogant and so power thirsty they cannot see the forest for the trees.

Keep in mind we only get a trickle of information to base our conclusions on. Imagine if we were flies on the wall and saw and heard what really goes on? There would be a collective pooping of the pants all across America. The fact is these people are stroking us. They act with the highest impunity and if you try to confront them...well you can't because they have expertly insulated themselves from the citizenry. When was the last time you were asked what you thought? Have you received a questionnaire in the mail or a phone call (other than the incessant phone calls during election time which are not meant to illicit your opinion) and asked what you feel about a certain legislator or pending legislation? I'll bet not.

What is so tragic is the legislative process attracts the best and the brightest but it is all for naught. If you look at their resumes and see that they are from good schools (in many cases great schools) and/or they come from well established families it creates hope. They politic during election time and blow incredible amounts of smoke up our as**s and the most pathetic part of that is we buy into it. It doesn't matter that political season after political season we are confronted with the same s**t and we always buy into it. And the excuse of going for the lesser of two evils is no longer valid because they are all equally evil. It doesn't matter what party they are aligned with and the proof is there every time when they get elected, go to work, and act in unison with all the existing buffoons. Yes I said buffoons. And I said that because I was being polite. They no longer have my respect so they are not shielded from the monikers that actually fit the description of what they do. I know there was a time in my life I would never chastise the office of a legislator and especially the office of the President. But as I grew older and paid more attention I came to the realization that these people are men and women just like us. What they have done differently than us is decide to enter the political life. When they do that a transformation occurs, which has yet to be defined, that changes them from a normal person into arrogant jerks that think their poop doesn't stink.

The best and the brightest get no respect because they don't deserve it.

PAULA DEEN SHOWS JUST HOW UNFORGIVING LIBERALS ARE

Alec Baldwin can make disparaging remarks to and about his daughter, berate airline officials for telling him to turn off his phone before a flight and spout homophobic remarks to a reporter for accusing his wife of tweeting during the funeral for James Galdofini and suffer no consequences. He can even promote the idea of running for Mayor of New York City. But when Paula Deen admits to racial slurs she made years ago, Hell hath no fury like a scorned liberal.

America no longer hides the fact we operate on the basis of the double standard. In fact, America has perfected the double standard. We claim we are a forgiving people but our actions say otherwise. Instead of coming forward and graciously accepting her apology, America (I mean liberal America), decided instead to plot a course that would result in the ruining of her life. Why? What would any group, liberal or conservative, really gain from this? Or was it to just "teach her a lesson." I know today, from the President down, from the highest seats of religion, to the powerful groups that continually fight for rights, not one representative stepped forward to say wait a minute let's think about what we are doing here. Should we really treat Paula Deen worse than the Gitmo prisoners?

These groups that would destroy a person's life for a

mistake they made years ago and apologized for, are making America out to be unforgiving. How do you not forgive Paula Deen but you can forgive a sitting United States President who got a blowjob from his mistress in the White House? And the guy will probably end up back in the White House as the First Gentleman.

Sometimes Americans are just tragically silly.

HAS JOHN McCAIN EVER MET A WAR HE DIDN'T LIKE?

Allow me to preface my remarks by stating the fact I have been a conservative thinker most of my adult life. I even supported John McCain at certain points in the past as I have with many conservatives. But now I am fed up with John McCain's constant and consistent need to get America into a war no matter where one happens to start. In fact, left to his own devices, he would create a war if he felt we needed it. In a way I can't blame him after what the North Vietnamese did to him. Unfortunately, we run the risk of taking that mindset too far like we did in Iraq because President Bush was pissed that Saddam Hussein tried to assassinate his father. The reasons we enter a war and prosecute a war must be based solely on the protection of the American people. If in that process we also create much needed military bulwarks to protect America's interests (including oil businesses) than so be it. But first and foremost, we protect American citizens.

My dissolution with John McCain started during the presidential election of 2008. I was a registered Republican at the time and was anxious to see our candidate get into the highest office in our land.

Unfortunately, he made two huge mistakes. The first mistake was choosing Sarah Palin as his running mate. Don't get me wrong I love the way Sarah Palin thinks but strategically, it was political suicide. The end result bears me out. Secondly, he was rather forthright in his assessment of the housing collapse in that he put the blame squarely on the shoulders of the American home buyer. And to make it worse, without hesitation he said there would be no bail out of homeowners from his Administration. Now despite the fact I am a conservative I was a conservative with a home that lost half its value. And even at that time it was being revealed that the housing collapse was more, if not all, the fault of the financial industry and the failure of regulators under the control of President Bush. Now, of course, we all know what really went on. And now all the perps are buying their way out of jail time by paying fines to the government. Ain't that nice.

Even though McCain lost the election he still won't go away. He remains a congressman and doing things I disagree with. Primarily his eagerness to enter into skirmishes around the world under the pretense of protecting our national interests with the oil trade among the most important obviously. And you have to question who he surrounds himself with that serve as advisers. In the 2008 election he chose as his running mate, Sarah Palin. If he was trying to win based on breaking new ground just as Obama was, it didn't work and wasn't a good idea because it just weakened his image. It was a gamble that didn't pay off.

If he operates as a war hawk and uses advisers whose advice is questionable, you have a disaster waiting to happen. I appreciate his service in the military but that can't serve as a reason to accept questionable judgment. The U.S. is involved in problem areas in too many parts of the world. We are spread too thin and the dollars aren't there with the economy still in the tank. Not to mention we are not effecting much change no matter where we are. The American model is not selling in the Middle East that's for sure.

The world is never going to have a shortage of tyrants. If every time one pops up we go after him we will be a nation constantly at war. That stretches our forces and runs up our costs. The prevailing approach in Washington right now should be diplomacy unless it is a direct attack on America. If a direct attack is the purpose of one of these tyrants we deal with it swiftly and decisively. But to get involved in everything deemed unjust is foolish.

We can't be the world's police department.

GUN CONTROL

It's happening again. This time it was a 20 year old man who killed his mother and then went to an elementary school and horrifically proceeded to kill 26 people which included 20 children. Not one person, whether a gun toting NRA disciple or a fanatical gun control liberal, can come away from this tragedy without feeling a deep sense of loss and unbridled sorrow. Whether it is a whack job in Norway or a freak in China or a nut job in America, they will find the weapon they need to kill because it is what they intend to do. A gun is not the only implement of death, it is one of numerous implements of death. The intent is to kill. The weapon(s) become a strategic choice. If they can't find a gun (if that is what they prefer) they will get a knife, poison, bomb, or any kind of weapon of destruction to get the job done. What are we going to do? Get rid of every gun, knife, or implement that can be used to create poison or a bomb?

What it really comes down to is both the proponents and opponents of gun control use these tragedies to further their cause. They are ambulance chasers. They don't really give a crap about the victims. They only see an opportunity to enrich themselves by getting people to accept their premise. Jumping up and down in a frenzy shouting see I told you so if guns didn't exist this never would have happened. Give me a break. Political discourse, if that's what this really is, has devolved into a pile of steaming crap evidenced by our last election. There are two sides wanting two starkly different things. What it comes down to is control. Each side wants to control the environment so that it pleases them. In all probability, and this is true of both sides, the environment they are promoting is based on bad science they created. People wouldn't die if we didn't have guns or we would be safer if more people had guns. All this is exacerbated by the presence of lawyers who decide what everyone should do or not do beginning with the Supreme Court. People watch as lawyers argue cases and based on their arguments we are then told what to do. It doesn't involve right or wrong it only comes down to who is the better lawyer, and more importantly, what is their political persuasion. This is how it works. A tragedy occurs and moments later Facebook and Twitter are flooded with comments about the incident. Politicians look at this and call the lawyers into action. The lawyers draw up a game plan designed to get their camp what they want. Now hold on I haven't even got to the media yet. In the event you live under a rock, lawyers, politicians, and the media truly believe we are idiots and the only way we survive is that our lives are led by them.

Now that is scary.

HOW INCREDIBLY RUDE WE ARE TO LEGAL IMMIGRANTS

Let me say from the outset, I do not support illegal immigration. I don't care what part of the world you come from; if you come here you should come here legally. I will also say it is embarrassing that America has not come up with a process agreeable to all parties so that people can come here and take advantage of the opportunities of this great country. Aside from that sentiment the point I would like to make with this article is that as a country made up of immigrants we can sure be rude to today's immigrants here legally. If you welcome a guest to your home you wouldn't be rude to them, would you? If an individual makes their home in this country legally with the hope of gaining citizenship one day then they are a welcomed guest in our home. Yet we trivialize them in too many ways.

Allow me to provide some background so that I may lend myself some credibility. I am a conservative white American male. I am engaged to marry a Hispanic who has a Green card. She is about to take the test for citizenship fulfilling a dream she has had for years. She waited years before finally getting up the nerve to do it. The reason she had to "get up the nerve" is because the way she has been treated as a Green card holder. She never felt worthy. Although she is here legally, pays taxes, obeys the law, and has raised four wonderful children who were born here, she has always been treated as a second class citizen. This treatment came from all quarters.

Conservatives, liberals, and even other Hispanics treated her as if she was not as good as them because she held a Green card. She came here for the opportunities America offered. She worked two menial jobs for minimum wage and paid her bills on time. The future was more for her children than her and she devoted her life to that. She raised them in the only area she could afford and despite the horrendous crime rate and sub-standard schools, she was able to steer them away from the gang life or any kind of criminal behavior. Her children flourished. One is a United States Marine, one works in law enforcement, another is a business owner hoping to give others a job, and the youngest one hopes to follow his sister into the Marines. Pretty damn good for a Green card holder wouldn't you say?

Now to get to my main beef. I have helped this wonderful woman study for her citizenship test. When I learned about the process to do this and viewed a sampling of the questions that will be asked, I almost threw up. I know it's the Federal Government and it is well documented that no institution or person could possibly waste money more than the Federal Government but even this caused me to pause. I just lied. It didn't cause me to pause instead it really pissed me off. Not only has this woman been a good American (minus the paperwork) who has worked hard, paid her taxes and raised children who serve our country and community, she did so without ever once complaining despite being treated as a second class citizen. Frankly, she should be allowed to walk into the Federal office that administers the citizenship test and instead of a test they should simply ask what took her so long and just have her sign and tell her how proud the government is to have her and her family. A family that strengthens this country by virtue of their very presence.

But instead she could be turned down because she may not be able to correctly answer questions like;

- ✓ The Federalist Papers supported the passage of the Constitution. Name one of the writers.
- ✓ During the Cold War, what was the main concern of the United States?

If you sent Jay Leno into the streets to ask those two questions of Americans born and raised here, chances are they would not have a clue.

What they should do and they should do it with all who apply for citizenship is have them come in and discuss with the interviewer how they have lived their lives as a resident of this country and ask them why they believe they would be good Americans. They would be overwhelmed by the numbers of good people that pass before them. It is offensive to treat a person with a Green card as someone less than you and it is also offensive to pin citizenship hopes on the chance that their memory will serve them well on that day they are asked one of those dumb-ass questions that most Americans couldn't answer. Do you really think citizenship should be determined by whether or not you can memorize the answers to these questions?

That should be for a mid-term quiz or something. How would correct or incorrect answers tell an interviewer if the person before them would be a good American?

THE KNOCKOUT GAME

Kids. What are you gonna do? Bored with real life kids have now come up with yet another way to fill their worthless days. It's not enough to kill and maim while sitting in a gaming chair at home, they feel the need to go out into the real world and wreak havoc. They attack innocent, unsuspecting victims while still suspended in this world of make believe. Either that or they are just complete a-holes.

The new game they are so fond of is walking up to their victim and sucker punching them. That's gotta be fun. It's called “the knockout game.” Kind of a clever name. They probably put more thought into that than what impact their game would have on unsuspecting victims.

This kind of thing has to make you wonder about the parents. Are they so oblivious to what their children are doing that they would release them into the world to do this kind of thing? Maybe they are down the street visiting the parents of the local bully? Barbarism has always been a feature of humankind but it is usually compartmentalized as opposed to being so widespread. A lack of decorum on American streets has become the norm but with this we have hit a new low. And the fact that these are kids makes it more frightening. What is going to feed their egos next once they get bored with this? And we know the judicial system is not going to right the problem because they can't right any problems. And the system's reputation for coddling the young is well deserved so a slap on the hand will be the most we can expect.

And you adults should keep in mind that if you defend yourself against a juvenile or even exact judgment of your own the same system that doesn't work will come after you frothing at the mouth like rabid dogs. You will be jailed and sued in a civil action.

So, in effect, you have to take the punch.

WE DON'T ALL HAVE AN AIDE NAMED FRAN TO TURN TO

Earlier today Vice President of the United States Joe Biden was at a sandwich shop buying lunch. In and of itself that sounds weird. Did they run out of food at his house? Anyway, he was short on cash so he turned to an aide named Fran and asked for $10 (we still have not determined if Fran actually gave him the $10). The food was for a weekly lunch meeting with the President of the United States of America.

So let me see if I have this correct. The president and vice president, and I imagine a few top level cabinet members (which means there was a number of millionaires in the room) are going to have lunch at the White House. They send the vice president out to buy lunch. Hmmm.

Okay, this is disconcerting on a number of different levels. Was this meant as a cutesy story and we didn't get all the details? Why would the Vice President, who has a contingent of Secret Service agents with him at all times, just take off to a local sandwich shop to grab a bite to eat for himself and the prez? Was it a PR stunt designed by the Vice President's office to endear him to the American public as being more like one of us? What about the White House chef who probably earns more than the prez? Was he/she sitting in the kitchen twiddling their thumbs? Or maybe the VP has become like all VP's and is just a butt monkey.

Doesn't he have more pressing business to attend to? Our economy (except for the 1%) still sucks. A lot of us don't have a Fran to turn to when we run out of money. And what about this comment about always paying what he owes? Was that meant as a slight because there are still a whole lot of Americans that would pay their bills if they could but they can't. He also said “In Delaware, you pay. It's simple." Really, why? Do people in Delaware get their legs broken if they don't pay? Do people in Delaware have more money? I'm not sure what that statement means. Maybe it is just Joe and his poor command of the language.

The media should know there are more important stories to report than this cutesy stuff that ain't so cute to some people.

ARE THE REPUBLICANS THE DUMBEST PEOPLE IN THE ROOM?

Before I registered as an Independent I was a Republican. Before I was a Republican I was a Democrat. I am running out of political parties. But in my rant here I want to focus on the Republicans because that would be my party of choice if they would just get their s**t together! As a youngster, because in America youngsters are allowed to vote, I was a Democrat probably because my high school teachers told me to be that. Since you can't tell the difference between high school teachers and college professors, I was a Democrat in college. Then came the real world in which I had to hold a job, raise a family, and keep that family safe from the bad guys. So I became a Republican. Isn't that what is suppose to happen when you grow up?

Unfortunately, the Republican party has refused to change with the times. I know among the Republicans there are some smart people, I think. But smart people can be dumb, just look at our current president. So where is this resistance to change in the Republican party coming from? Are the money changers refusing to allow the change? Are they threatening to pull the financial plug. I am sure that is part of the reason. Are the Republicans so far removed from everyday folks that they couldn't relate if their lives depended on it? Or do they just not give a crap?

Whatever the reason or reasons the party must address them now! The Democrats are driving a bulldozer across the country plowing under every conservative bastion still in existence. Sure, Republicans talk about it day and night so we know they know. But talk is cheap. I know how hard it is to accept change. I am turning 62 and, believe me, I have had change forced down my throat since “the good old days.” But I accepted it because I had to and so does the Republican party. They can toe the line if they want but they are going to have to accept losses at every turn. I am the last person who wants the Democrats to have complete control. I live in California and I have first hand experience with that. The Democrats have totally f**ked up California and the pseudo Republican Arnold Schwarzenegger was no help.

Voters are looking for something different in these times and if Republicans want to give them the same old s**t, different day routine, they are going to wither away. It's already started. Gone will be any kind of diversity of opinion and it will simply be the Democrat opinion. Gag me. Minus Obamacare we have limited the damage Obama, Reid, and Pelosi have done but elections are on the horizon and conservatives need to ready themselves for the battle. Conservatives need to understand that this generation does not hold sacred what past generations held sacred. Back in the day there was no social media but now it rules the day. Obama even got half the baby boomer vote. Republicans cannot live on seniors alone. And they certainly can't help their senior constituencies if they are not elected. Duh.

We don't always like change but it is inevitable. Either you go with it or you get left behind. Right now it appears they are getting left behind.

HORSE DUNG

When I see articles with headlines like “Oil price falls as Iran deal eases supply fears”, the first word I think of is horse dung. Don't ask me why, I don't own a horse and I don't even plan to ride a horse, ever! It just seems like an appropriate word to explain my reaction to these bogus headlines that even a crackhead knows is horse dung. There are no oil supply fears. I have no fear that we are running low on oil. The guys that control the oil have no fear because they know there is no shortage. In fact, everyone knows there is no shortage so why would anyone have any fear? There is maybe 3 people in the world that would buy into this statement so why even waste the space. Just be honest and say oil may go up or oil may go down because Iran will now be able to sell their oil on the open market but the bottom line is the people who *manipulate* oil prices will make the final decision. There is plenty of oil out there and now there will be even more with Iran's so chances are prices will go down. But don't try to blow smoke up my behind talking about ”supply fears.” Where the f**k do they get these writers?

I'm to that point , and I'm sure many others are, that I just want the yanking of my chain, stopped. When oil prices are up don't tell me an oil refinery shut down half way across the world and it caused a spike in pricing. And don't tell me that prices are down because there is a glut of oil on the market. Just don't tell me anything because when I go to the pump I think only one thing and that is that I am being screwed by the oil conglomerates. And it's true. Everyone knows it's true. Making up bogus reasons for oil's up and down activity is just an insult to our intelligence. Just screw us and be on your way.

Most of us down here in the real world are aware. We are not stupid. We know that getting screwed by government and big business (is that redundant?) is an everyday reality we can't change. We vote people in and out of elected positions but when they are there they are owned by special interests. We know this. When large public corporations announce their quarterly figures we don't pay attention because we know they're making money. On the following day the multi-million dollar bonuses are announced and we see that. We accept what we can't control but we still reserve the right to complain.

We know the arrangement between everyday Americans and government/big business is that you will do what you have the power to do, make your money, and then you will throw us a bone. So what is important here is what kind of a bone you are going to toss us and how you toss it. Be respectful and show some appreciation. You are where you are because of us. At times give us more than we expect. And when times are hard limit how much you take from us. Don't ever blame us for what happens because you are in control not us. We won't take credit for the good times so don't blame us for the bad times. When we do things you don't approve of (do you hear me Neil Cavuto?) don't say anything because you do crap everyday that we don't approve of. You are in control so if we do something you don't think is right in your twisted mind don't blame us. Someone at the controls screwed up.

PAKISTAN, A DANGEROUS ALLIANCE

Imran Khan, a former cricket player turned politician, is placing the United States in a very precarious position solely for his political aspirations. When combining his need for attention with his hatred of America the result is a threat that must be dealt with or people will die. Personally, I could give a s**t about Pakistan. I see them as a country of whackos like so many of their Middle East neighbors. Their governments are corrupt and their citizens are destitute because of it. Like all of the Middle East it is a hotbed of anger and hatred. Hatred mostly for America. The problem, for America, is that those whackos have nuclear capability. And they are in a region that also includes countries that enjoy undeserved stability only as long as their dictators have complete control. I obviously mean China and Russia. Both China and Russia (our pseudo friends) have nuclear capability and are afraid of us. China counters that with the purchase of the majority of our national debt and Russia...likes to talk s**t. They know that a nuclear confrontation with us would be disastrous for the entire world so they don't do what would be the dumbest thing known to mankind.

But Pakistan, that's a different story. Sometimes you have to be friends with someone you don't really like but it is in the best interests of everyone. Keep your friends close but your enemies closer. Even a crackhead knows that Iran controls everything that goes on in that part of the world when it comes to the Islamist state. In terms of nuclear capability I am more concerned about Pakistan than Iran. If you recall it was a Pakistani scientist who set up his own personal swap meet to peddle the nuclear capability to any and all takers. But our presence in the region is a deterrent so that doesn't occur again. Or else Iran would simply call Pakistan and order a bomb from them and they would pay for the shipping and handling costs. Like ordering from the Christmas catalog of your favorite retailer.

So something as simple as a up and coming politician looking for attention can upset the balance of power. He doesn't pause to look at the bigger picture but instead does things that could have disastrous results. He has outed our CIA station chief in Pakistan. He claims it was for the purpose of ending drone strikes in his country but the truth is he is using that issue to advance his political career. He said he was “punishing” the CIA for a drone strike in an area his political party controls. He also mobilized the party faithful to block NATO supply lines to Afghanistan after a drone attack killed Pakistani Taliban leader Hakimullah Mehsud. Khan has asked for military action against the Pakistani Taliban to cease.

Okay, now the picture becomes more clear. How do you say puppet? This guy is obviously the front man for the Pakistani Taliban. He says as much in his own declarations. Unfortunately, it's guys like this and countries like Pakistan that keep us in the thick of things. Otherwise, we would have to control activities in that region from afar and in doing so would probably inflict more damage because the bottom line is you can't f**k with the biggest and baddest nation on earth.

We have a major problem with the Pakistanis having the nuclear capability and the terrorists who would like to steal it or get it by gaining control of the country. If you can imagine an Iran having this same capability the world would be up s**t creek without a paddle. Hence the effort by the United States to keep Iran from enriching plutonium. It is not a position I want us in but it is a position we are forced to be in.

IRAQ'S PREDICTABLE REQUEST FOR WEAPONS

If anyone in Washington has learned from our experience in the Middle East then Iraq's recent request for assistance will not be heard. Iraq says it needs weaponry due to the internal strife they blame on a resurgent terror threat due in part to both the conflict in neighboring Syria and the Arab Spring. Well, maybe they should have thought about that before giving us the boot. Remember, we could not come to an agreement regarding the immunity issue of our troops so we left. And also you will recall the obscene amounts of money and weapons that we provided while in country that we can't freakin' find. A good portion of that money and those weapons are surely in the hands of the Iranians. Even that crackhead you just tripped over would know that. But that's what you get when you let Al-Qaeda do the accounting. We have maybe three officials who could wildly speculate where all of the weapons and money went so any requests now and in the future, have to be denied. A memo should also be sent to both the Democrats and Republicans reminding them that the people over there cannot vote in our elections so don't think about providing more aid to buy votes.

Just as we should not have been in Vietnam, we should not be in the Middle East. Why these non-military types in Washington want to keep getting involved in losing propositions is beyond me. I am not against war, I am against where and how we do it. We will always have war as long as men want to kill each other over whatever reason is believable at the time. You don't bring a knife to a gunfight. When the United States goes over to the Middle East burdened with endless rules on how our soldiers fight and they confront an enemy that has absolutely no rules, it is bringing a knife to a gunfight. That's a set-up. Shame on us.

Since right after WWII the Middle Eastern nations have been playing us as well as all the other willing super powers. If they ask us for guns and money for A, B, and C, they are going to use those guns and money for D, E, and F.

If you don't believe me go back to that crackhead you tripped over and ask him.

CREDIBILTY, WE DON'T NEED NO STINKIN' CREDIBILITY

America is the biggest and the baddest. We are the most free. We are the most prosperous. We offer greater opportunities to everyone (legal or not). We are the most generous. We are the fairest in every regard. We are protected by an incredible Constitution. So why are we so freaking worried about credibility? Every country that enjoys some semblance of a democratic system strive to make that system like ours. And those countries that are ruled by an iron hand are ruled by an iron hand because its people want what we have and the only way the rulers can keep them down is dictatorially. We just witnessed Syria's dictator gas 1400 or more of his own citizens just to keep them from having the freedom they deserve. The kind of freedom we enjoy every day. No, what needs to happen is everyone else needs to show us they are credible. I am so tired of hearing that we need to do this or that we need to do that because our credibility is on the line. On the line with who? Pick a country that if we don't have credibility with them we will somehow collapse. There isn't one. Most countries need us and the rest fear us. When another country is in trouble the first one they think of is America. When another country is screwing up the first one they think of is America because we will be knocking on their door. We are the world's police and we are the world's welfare system. And those European countries who are scoffing at that last statement, my question to you is why do we always need to come over and fix the crap that occurs in your neighborhood? Syria is a problem and they are right down the street from you. Fix it!

Every time the President or a legislator speaks of credibility I cringe. When they do that they make America sound weak. Oh gee, we better be careful in this situation or we will compromise our credibility. Bull s**t. Personally, I don't care what other countries think of us. I am only concerned about what we think of them. Every country wants something from us. They want money or trade or protection. Or if they are an enemy they want us to leave them alone. They all want something from America. So it stands to reason we need to see some credibility on their part.

When America has a problem do we call someone else for help? No. If you retort that China props up our economy I will answer that we open investment in America to anyone. China just happens to be our biggest investor.

Our root problem is that we spend too much but that's a political problem and we baby our politicians when we should probably tar and feather them. The fact is America doesn't need anyone. We don't have to worry about credibility. We became a worldwide economy and a worldwide this and a worldwide that only because corporations wanted to make ungodly profits. We are equipped in this country to do everything ourselves. I am not an isolationist but know that if we had to survive we could do it without any outside help. So take your credibility and pound sand.

A SLIPPERY SLOPE TO BE SURE

We are now seeing the frightening political aftermath of a foreign policy that has been in free fall for decades. Since we initially engaged in the affairs of the Middle East it has been one disaster after another. Political jockeying for strategic position in a land that became the birthplace of the superpowers was about to begin. After WWII, the Middle East was set upon by the United States and the Soviet Union in a dual quest to gain control. The area was a cornucopia of resources and in political disarray. Oil and the new nation of Israel meant we were going to be there for the long haul. The Soviet Union also saw the potential in the region's rich supply of oil. After a forced cooperation in WWII the United States and the Soviet Union resumed the hostile relations that were present before the war. To say the war emboldened both nations is a understatement.

Both sides were able to claim victory and the chest thumping began. In a burgeoning industrial world oil was gold. The attack at Pearl Harbor by Japan was precipitated by an oil embargo put in place by the United States. That is not the complete answer to why Japan attacked the United States but it is part of the answer. It simply highlights the importance of oil at that time and how the Middle East was viewed as so strategic. America's involvement in WWII created an opportunity, if you will, in that since we just spent several years engaged in that area of the world, why not set up shop? We wanted oil, the Middle East had lots of oil, and we could stay at our friend's house (Israel) since we happened to be in the neighborhood. It seemed to be a perfect fit except the Soviet Union wasn't warming to the idea. They didn't necessarily want people like us moving into the neighborhood. Since there was a power vacuum in the region created by a lack of Arab nationalism it was an easy target for both the United States and the Soviet Union. Now remember the Soviet Union at that time was a Communist Empire (is it still?) and we know how the United States felt about "commies." So to make a long story short the United States and the Soviet Union went to work gaining as much control as possible to enhance their new found designations as superpowers. Boys will be boys. The fractured leadership in that area saw an opportunity and immediately started playing the two powers against one and another to gain as many favors as possible (nothing has changed obviously).

Fast forward to 2013 and the Syrian gassing of its own people. The Soviet Union is now Russia and run by an ego maniacal left-over relic from the cold war. The United States is being run by a President and Legislature that doesn't know how to spell the words foreign policy. The same conditions exist in the area that existed after WWII. We both want the oil and we still have sleep-overs in Israel. Back to Syria gassing its own people. It isn't hard to make an argument to send bombs in to remind Assad that the world agreed to refrain from the use of chemical weapons. Unfortunately, Russia, and it's ex-KGB leader suffering from a Napoleonic Complex, has just created a very dangerous wrinkle in the fabric of the situation. He has notified the world in his usual eloquent way that if the United States fires missiles at Damascus, Russia may step in to protect Assad. Since Russia has sent warships over to the same area where we have warships, we should take this seriously. Is Putin dumb enough to start a war between superpowers and give the world WWIII? Sure. Think about the present and the kinds of leaders in charge of countries that are capable and willing to wage war against the United States. A former KGB officer with an outsized ego and a pea brain, a 28 (we think) year old kid running North Korea who just executed his former girlfriend, any number of radical Islamists running any number of countries or groups, and of course, the Supreme Leader of Iran who wouldn't blink twice if he fired a nuke at Israel.

So maybe it is time to realize that despite how powerful the United States is, if the bad guys have a death wish we could be in deep doodoo. If I take a gun to a knife fight but the guy with the knife stabs me in the back, then it really didn't matter that I was such a bad-ass now does it? If Russia supports a leader like Assad who is willing to murder his own people then it stands to reason Putin is okay with that. Right? I understand the importance of oil reserves and the protection of them. I understand the importance of establishing strategic placements of military bulwarks. But if we continue to do these two things while at the same time countries that don't like us become more emboldened, we may have to switch game plans. The standard response of stop that crap or we will bomb you has seen its day. This is not any longer about weakness and strength. We are seeing weak countries win battles because of this death wish thing. It is about being smarter. Remember this, countries that engage in war or killing indiscriminately use as their warriors young men and women usually not old enough to drink legally or, in some countries, child soldiers while they direct their actions from the confines of a leather chair in an opulent office.

We live in a world that experiences unbelievable innovations in technology, medicine, education, etc. but when it comes to resolving disputes we use the age old method of killing each other. Now at some point, due to the aforementioned innovations in technology, we will eventually blow each other to smithereens. Does that make sense? If in 2013 any kid can go to the internet and find instructions on how to build a dirty bomb, well...you do the math. One way we may be able to make change is if we take the politicians out of the mix and replace them with today's best innovators. The innovators obviously have incredible minds and make a habit of thinking outside of the box. The problem of course is the egos of the politicians. The egos that keep them mounted on their high horses.

America is historic for putting into office the guy who has the best line of bull s**t. But bull s**t will never stop us from killing each other. For the sake of our children and their children and all future generations to come, we need to stop the killing. We are sliding down a slippery slope right now with Russia and its whacked out leadership. This is no time to call the little guy's bluff and we won't gain anything by bombing Syria anyway. It hasn't worked elsewhere and it won't work in Syria.

YOU'RE ALL A BUNCH OF DODO BIRDS

I actually wanted to say something a lot worse but would not be able to get this piece into print if I did. So I will settle for dodo bird. The bungling, flightless bird that kind of looks like Harry Reid. So, obvious to all, I am talking about Washington. And I mean all of Washington. There is no more aisle as I see it. One party is no better than the other. And if I hear another politician talk about credibility, I am going to vomit! We have Socialist Europe and Communist China chiding us to get our act together regarding the budget. So don't talk to me about credibility. We ain't got no stinkin' credibility. Washington has made a laughing stock of America. And to add insult to injury, they really think we the citizens believe one group is responsible over the other. All of you from the President down are at fault. There is no good guy in the equation. You are all a bunch of dodo birds. You're pathetic.

What I don't understand is that you have no shame. Aren't you even a little embarrassed by your behavior? I know I am. For crying out loud, you're all highly educated. Why can't, or won't, you do your job? You are polling at ridiculous numbers. People are fed up with your crap. And still, you drag this thing on and hurt the nation as a result. You should be fired! If you had any self-respect, you would resign. In the private sector you would not be able to keep your job because it is performance based. As elected officials you are not performing. You are not even doing a crappy job. You are not doing your job at all. When the American, and otherwise, voter put you in office they entrusted you to do a certain kind of job that would result in this nation advancing after enduring a horrific economy that ruined the lives of many. And what have you done? Nada, nothing, zero, zip. Whatever term you choose to use, you have done absolutely nothing! Wait, I digress, you have done something. You've screwed up! And in your twisted logic you would say at least you've done something as if screwing up is better than not doing anything. It's time to buck up boys and girls. Earn your money because there is no chance you will earn respect.

The only difference between the dodo bird and Washington is the dodo bird is extinct. Well, we can always hope.

OBAMA AND HIS HOUSE OF CARDS

Obama has pulled the political card, the excuse card, the pity card, the transference card, the poor people card, the race card, the guilt card and so it begs the question what other cards is he holding? Depending on the crowd he is addressing he will adjust his speech accordingly. He plays to the crowd. Forget that we want our presidents to act presidential. That's not the Chicago politics style. If he is speaking to a black crowd he will start (his version anyway) talking like a brother. This dude is so far from being a "brother" he couldn't be one if he tried. When he is talking to Democrats he demonizes Republicans and in the process forgets they are American citizens he represents. And out comes the excuse card if the poop hits the fan.

Whatever happened it couldn't possibly be his fault. It's always someone else. If something happens outside the United States out comes the transference card. America will help, maybe, but we will lead from behind. If we are to be the biggest and the baddest you can't lead from behind. Any self-respecting gang leader knows that. The President did this with Syria and it allowed that little person in Russia to step to center stage. And when it comes to the poor people card there is no end to his quest to take every penny he can get from the working man. Why create jobs when you can just use the taxpayers money and provide a poor person with a comfortable lifestyle? And if you complain he will pull out two cards. The pity card and the guilt card. Because you should feel guilty if you don't have pity on the less fortunate. And with those two cards he will go after the wealthy because, after all, they didn't build their success by themselves. Somebody helped them. I'm trying to build a business and I ain't getting any freaking help from anyone. Tell me where these helpers are because I got no shame, I'll let them help me. And I'm still flabbergasted that our President pulled the race card when he took to the podium in support of Trayvon Martin. When Zimmerman was found not guilty did the President step back up to the podium and say, my bad. This President is throwing out these cards like he's a blackjack dealer in Atlantic City (we know he doesn't like Vegas). I just don't see this as presidential. What happened to equal representation? What happened to the buck stops here? What happened to leadership?

Update: I didn't even have time to upload this article and he did it again. He pulled out the transference card when speaking to nearly 4000 at the Navy Yard Memorial Service. He dropped the gun control debate right in the lap of America. He said we didn't care enough and that is why we didn't attack the gun control issue in exactly the way he wanted to attack it. Mr. President it does shock us and we do want a transformation. We have been asking for that all along. We want the guns out of the hands of the bad guys and the mentally disabled but instead you want to take the guns out of the hands of law abiding citizens.

If you are keeping America safe how did the Navy Yard shooter get past security? And what about crime in America? Are you keeping us safe from that? Have you been to Chicago lately? Maybe you should put a television in your golf cart so you can watch the news? Don't blame America. Blame yourself and the inept Congress. What the f**k are you guys doing in Washington? Before they even found the shooter you were on television bitching about someone else not fixing the budget. Mr. President, do you ever do anything wrong? Is anything ever your fault? Or is it just that the rest of us are so f**ked up? Is arrogance spelled with two r's?

America does want gun control. We want to control the guns so they don't get into the hands of thugs and whack jobs. Because if you and Congress don't do your jobs then we have to fend for ourselves. Stop worrying so much about our credibility worldwide, worry more about your credibility right here at home!

P.S. Stop turning every event into a political soapbox.

WHAT THE WORLD IS WITNESSING

It happened with Jimmy Carter and we didn't learn from it. What Carter did to this nation took years to mend and we seem to have lost our memory of it. Well, what we are seeing today should jog our memory. The players are different but the scenarios are uncanny in their likeness. Our economic strength is weakened by massive debt, our Middle East policy is laughable, employment continues to lag, the Administration and Congress are hopelessly ineffective, socialism is on the rise again, and we are getting stroked at the gas pump. But lest you get too depressed the stock market is raging. Unfortunately, it appears to benefit only the One Percent as evidenced by recent studies on the accumulation of wealth.

It took Ronald Reagan on his white horse to ride in and save the day almost as if it was scripted by Hollywood. Unfortunately, the Republican Party is so fragmented today that any hope of a Ronald Reagan is a pipe dream. The hard core refuse to come into the 21st century, the Libertarians who reside in the party are becoming stronger, the Tea Party is disruptive, and there are too few young conservatives with a centrist bent. A dear friend once told me that like it or not I have to accept the changes that are occurring around me. I am an older conservative that resisted these changes until my friend showed me how I was pissing in the wind. I reluctantly agreed to accept the fact that change was inevitable but I don't have to accept how it is occurring today.

I do want a stronger economy but I want it through creation of American jobs, a resurgence of a manufacturing sector, and control of our debt. I do want to reduce the debt but not by creating money and borrowing from the communists. I do want to get out of these wars that have gone on too long but I don't want to retreat with a whimper like a wounded puppy. I do want to maintain credibility in the world and not get cuffed around by a height challenged ex-KGB agent. I do want the political infighting to stop but I want innovation of thought from those Yale and Harvard grads that occupy Congress and the White House. I don't want socialism because it is counter to personal freedom but I do want to go to the doctor and not be charged $30,000 to have a bunion removed. And I would like greater diversity in the types and costs of fuel I consume so I am not at the mercy of an uncaring, greedy CEO of an oil company who will raise the price of a gallon of gas if someone farts in Bangladesh.

America is becoming the butt of a bad joke. I am not so dumb that I don't realize the world is run by those with the money. It has always been the case and always will be. Money translates into power so the power goes to those with the largest bank accounts. The accumulation and maintenance of wealth occurs on a worldwide basis. There are no borders when it comes to this process. So if a corporation or an individual is in a financial arrangement outside of the United States he/she or it will be beholden to the desires and whims of that country. This is understandable to a point. If it becomes a situation that results in the weakening of our nation's economy or presents a threat to our national security, then our Administration in concert with Congress has to pull on the reins. This is where we run into a problem. While these corporations and individuals are beholden to these foreign countries where they do business, the Administration and Congress is beholden to the Corporations and individuals. This is squarely the result of the phenomenon of lobbying.

It has always been understood that politicians rely on the uninformed voter. It is included in every Political Science 101 class. The uninformed voter will have little or no understanding of the lobbying process. The lobbying process is at the core of every decision that comes out of Washington. It matters not that the education levels of our politicians are extraordinary, the decisions are made for them. The coordinating efforts between the politicians and the lobbyists are also extraordinary. It is a fine tuned and detailed process that has withstood many attempts to dismantle it. Unfortunately, you cannot dismantle something that serves both political parties. You can have a vocal opponent like former Senator Paul but if he can only get a few people on his side he will always be wholly outnumbered. So at the end of the day it is the lobbyist who has the politician's ear and not the voter. The resulting decisions have to be accepted because no alternative exists.

The voter, in essence, has become an afterthought. The lobbyists don't care about anyone but their client. The client is their lifeblood. The lobbyists love the money and the power. So the best we can hope for is for the corporations, wealthy individuals, lobbyists, and politicians to remember they too are Americans. And if things get too screwed up, they will also suffer.

When we have multiple problems both domestically and internationally it begs the question of whether or not the lobbying process is out of balance. If a little tyrant like Putin can step to center stage and actually look good despite screwing over his own people on a daily basis, then something is wrong. I didn't want to bomb Syria but we probably should have done it within the first 48 hours because the decision not to is now biting us in the butt.

The President talks often and freely about our credibility. I really don't support the argument because I don't really care what others think of us. But if we are concerned about credibility then we have to stop hurting ours. This is our fault. It is our fault because of the policies we create and maintain that are just not good. We saw what Carter did. Why are we doing it again? Listen people, we don't have a Ronald Reagan in the wings to step in and save us so matters are going to get even worse if we don't do something now.

MAYOR BLOOMBERG, PLEASE SHUT UP

Okay, I get it. You're rich and famous. And you seem to know what is best for us. You tell us we need to drink smaller sodas and give up our guns. And today you have informed us of a racist in our midst by re-defining what racism is. I get it. What I get is you are quite possibly the most arrogant person currently occupying this earth. When you came out branding Mr. de Blasio as a racist your reasoning was beyond suspect, it was just plain stupid. You said he brought out his bi-racial son as a way to get votes. You said it would compare to you saying you were Jewish to get the Jewish vote. Give me a moment here to catch my breath. Are you freaking serious?

First of all, who really cares? If voters didn't outwardly declare it they certainly feel inwardly that they prefer someone, and I don't know how to say this in the politically correct way, who is one of their own. Are you going to tell me that we didn't see many more blacks than usual come out to vote when Obama ran for president? Are you going to tell me more women didn't come out to participate when Hillary ran for President? Are you going to tell me you didn't get almost all the Jewish vote? And to add to that you are a registered Republican who behaves like a Democrat so you got the Jewish vote from both sides. Now before you ever ran for political office you were well know for your financial prowess so name recognition wasn't a problem. Had that not been the case, and knowing your mouth, I am convinced you would have campaigned pointing out the fact you are Jewish. Since you didn't have to do that, for obvious reasons I won't mention now because I don't want the Political Correctness police at my door, you feel you can accuse others of doing it. So while you say Bill de Blasio is a racist, I say you are a hypocrite.

This whole thing has made me thirsty. I'm going to holster my pistol and go get a Big Gulp. Oh yeah, I'm a white guy!

POLITICAL INERTIA

At this moment the world is witnessing the worst kind of political inertia imaginable. While world leaders are playing politics, people are dying. And dying the worst kind of death. Death by dictatorship. Syria is killing its children while the world sits idly by and does nothing. And the most powerful nation, our own America, is not leading the way. There is only one explanation and it should be obvious even to the dumbest of the dumb, it's politics. Even though both sides of the aisle pretty much agree we should drop some bombs somewhere, they can't agree on where, how many, and when. Meanwhile do you think the killing has stopped? Do you think maybe Assad is busily preparing to limit the damage? Hello! Is anyone home? It doesn't require an abundance of brain power to figure this one out.

Personally, I don't think we should drop any bombs anywhere, at least not now, and instead figure out some other approach. I admit to being a bit conservative but I'm tired. I'm tired of war that accomplishes nothing. I have a kid in the Marines and another preparing to sign up. I don't want them gassed in the streets of Damascus. Washington is saying no to boots on the ground and I am saying at my age I've been around a few blocks so don't blow smoke up my you know what.

With the President at an approval rating of less than 50%

and Congress struggling to hit 15% I am not feeling warm and fuzzy. With the UN being impotent and Russia being led by a former KGB officer and China run by communists we may have to call Fiji and ask them to make a decision for us. I do know that killing more people isn't going to help and the evidence bears me out on that. If all nations agree chemical warfare against a country's own people is beyond horrendous then all nations should, for the moment, set aside their differences and march into Assad's office and lay down the law. They just need to say they are going to collectively cut him off if he doesn't surrender his chemical weapons and then step down so the bloodshed will stop. If they want to stick around until a caretaker government is set up that may be advantageous. Once this is done they can all go back to hating each others guts for the most ridiculous reasons and the world can rest knowing everything is back to normal. The world will have resolved a major issue, no more children will die, and our leaders can return to their normal duties that get them such low approval ratings.

Now that is easy enough to not really hurt the brain, right? I mean, we don't want to overdo the thinking thing. After all, why go through all the years of college at prestigious universities only to think too much about stuff. Take a break. Relax. You obviously don't care about things like approval ratings or else you might do something to improve them. I will leave all the world leaders with one small nugget of wisdom. Don't bite the hand that feeds. In the event all the leaders of the world have forgotten, you work for us.

Time to go to work.

PRESIDENT OBAMA AND OPM

The Obamacare website is the latest example of how President Obama uses OPM. For those of you who abide under rocks, OPM is the acronym for Other Peoples Money. It is primarily used in a business setting but President Obama has expanded and extended its use to pretty much anything. He's like a shopaholic. If he sees something he likes, he buys it. He refuses to check the balance, in what he thinks is his personal account, and goes through with whatever he is buying at the moment. Presently he is purchasing political goodwill (that's my way of saying he is buying votes) and a political legacy. He wants to be remembered as the Chief Executive that finally brought national health care to America, forced the banking industry to its knees, and got us out of the protracted wars in the Middle East but instead his legacy will be one of running up the debt to historical levels, bringing socialized medicine to a free enterprise system, making us the laughing stock on the international stage, and further aggravating an already fractured relationship between Republicans and Democrats.

The company the White House hired to fix the debacle that is Obamacare has a questionable track record and we paid it 93 million dollars for a website that now may end up costing a billion dollars. No worries. Just print the money and get it done. This is what he does. He throws money at a problem believing that is what will work and despite failures of that approach he is not deterred. They say money talks and bull s**t walks. The President and his collection of rocket scientists thought the saying was money talks and bull s**t works.

Perhaps a typo is at the root of this approach?

I THINK NOT

The EU today issued a statement that the recent NSA spying debacle (and I am in no way defending the NSA) may affect the intelligence gathering cooperation because of "concerned Europeans." Right. Does the EU really think "Americans" are going to buy that crap. This statement is coming out of the EU offices and probably from a low level staff member. Or did they go out into the streets of Europe and actually ask the citizenry what they really think? I think not. Of those citizens who legitimately understand what is going on out there only a few would want their private security force to go away.

That's what America is to all these countries; a private security force. So they should shut up or put up. If we leave are they going to sufficiently guard themselves better than the baddest nation on the planet does? I think not. That's like a handful of Japanese anti-war protesters demanding we get our military forces out of their country. So they want to deal with China and North Korea themselves? I think not. When was the last time we invited any of you over to America to help keep us safe? So much of your world is safe and prosperous because of the greatest military might and the largest economy known to mankind. What don't you understand here? We went into Iraq and Afghanistan to clean that mess up and now that we are pretty much out of there, how are they doing? Do you suppose they are better off without us? I think not.

Myself and a lot of my countrymen would probably be all right with pulling out of all the countries we provide security to. It would save a boat load of money we could spend on ourselves. We have enough technology now, and are gaining more each day, that we can conduct war with anyone from my living room. It would require that every liberal in America would have to get their shorts out of a bunch and I have no doubt they would when a threat is right in their face.

European leaders speak to a “lack of trust” which is another hollow statement because no country fully trusts another. It's a forced cooperation and that is understood. Allies united in a common goal are doing so because it is in the best interests of their respective countries. I would be very nervous if we had “complete” trust in anyone. If we are going to help out another country you're damn right we are going make sure we don't get stabbed in the back. So if we decide to keep an eye on things, deal with it.

The option is you would have to take care of all of the problems that happen to be generated by your own neighbors. Do you want to take care of the problems in your neighborhood without the might of the United States of America? I think not.

FRIEND OR FOE?

How would we know? Let's imagine for a moment that we were totally isolated from the outside world. Let's say we were dependent on an information flow that was controlled by sources other than ourselves. Do you think the information would be in it's purest form of would we be receiving some adulterated form of it? Of course it wouldn't be pure and the extent of the adulteration would vary from one unreliable source to another.

So this is where the conversation should begin. It is absurd for us to not know what the unpredictable and dangerous world has in store for the United States. Even the hard core left must capitulate to this premise. Now that it has come out that the NSA has bugged everything and everyone imaginable, including you and I, where do we go from here? Obviously, or so it seems at the moment, we have gone too far. But how far should we go? And for you ultra privacy freaks don't try to portray the rest of the world as not having done some version of the same thing. That would be tantamount to saying the leaders of other world powers are responding as if they would never do such a thing. They are not because they know they are doing something too. Russia was just accused of bugging gift bags at the G20 Summit.

The bottom line is probably this; every major world power that has any intelligence/technical capability is going to be looking at the rest of the world. At the top of that list you will find the United States. You don't think China and Russia want to peek into our daily lives? And yes, our friends would want to as well. What has happened with the NSA scandal is we were uncovered and not the others. Thanks a bunch Eric Snowden. He may be a hero to some but not to me. I am not saying it didn't need to be revealed but it should have been done in a different manner. The problem with guys like Eric Snowden is that they have weak self-esteem and so this is also part individual because he needs to fill some void in his personal life. But living in exile in Russia makes it appear his plan backfired. Tough s**t buddy!

Since it was us rather than China or Russia that was uncovered what did you think the blow-back would be? We are the biggest, baddest, greatest nation in the world so if some guy in Des Moines farts it is front page news. We just happen to do everything better than everybody else. I for one, am not going to apologize for that.

But I am sure Obama is because he does that. He apologizes. He probably jumped on the phone, acted as if he didn't know, blamed it on someone else, and then told the other world leaders we will tone it down. He couldn't tell them we would stop because they do it too so telling them we would stop would be a bold faced lie.

And the fact is Obama, and although I am not a big fan,

didn't start this. It was started a really long time ago. It just became more sophisticated as technology advanced. And it is not a political thing because Democrats and Republicans both participated. Maybe we can let the two and a half Libertarians off the hook because they don't even believe we should have a government in any form. We will be hurt by this for a little while but then things will return to normal. If there is such a thing as normal. The countries we bugged are not going to let their economies collapse because it is a global economy, or let go of the military protection we provide, or want us to close our doors to legal or illegal migration because people love to live here. They will bitch and moan but all the while they know they are doing it too.

Just check the next container of money the Chinese send over to cover our debt and see if it isn't bugged!

IS IRAN PLAYING US?

Israel says they are. I don't know of any other country that monitors more closely, the activities in Iran. Sometimes we need to call an expert and Israel would be that expert. The latest article in the news is that Iran is removing anti-American posters. Things are happening in Iran there is no doubt about that. With the upcoming negotiations to slow down the uranium enrichment processes Iran is accused of being engaged in, we can't help but be hopeful. But the bottom line is, we are probably being played. Iran, or any other Middle Eastern country for that matter, has given every reason to not trust them and none to trust them.

Ever since the end of WWII when we decided to cozy up to, or control depending on your viewpoint, the Middle East, we have been played. At the time we went in so did the Soviet Union. And they were played too. It's how it works over there. It was that way after WWII and it is that way today. It is a strategy the Middle East has used effectively this entire time.

They have what we want, oil, and we have what they want, cash. And so I suppose it is a reasonable trade off but with Iran it is an entirely different matter. It must be that Iran's citizens are finally so hungry they're going to be dropping dead in the streets so even in Iran you will start seeing the internal problems we now see in Syria and

Egypt. The ruling clerics are strong but not invincible. At the end of the day they are only men. At some point the people will rise up even in Iran. History tells us that. So what Iran is doing now is exactly what Israel says they are doing. They are playing us. We have already raved about their cooperation at the outset of nuclear negotiations and Obama has asked Congress to withhold sanctions to give negotiations a chance.

How is it that smart people can be so dumb? I always thought that as a by-product of increasing one's intelligence it would decrease one's gullibility. Not so with Washington. Harvard, Yale, Stanford it doesn't matter where they received their degree they wouldn't know a scam if it bit them in the butt. So we will ease the sanctions on Iran, they will get plenty of business for their oil, we will send them cash and food and they will continue with a covert operation to build a bomb to wipe out Israel. They will get help from Russia to build a rocket that will have the capability to carry a nuclear warhead to the United States.

Great job Washington!

THE TEFLON PRESIDENT

Is anything this guy's fault? Seriously. The buck doesn't stop anywhere near him apparently. When I think of the President I can't help but think of John Gotti, the Teflon Don. No matter what type of event, whether big or small, that occurs and could have a negative impact on the President, it's not his fault. Has he actually taken blame for anything other than the losses of the two opponents in each of his races? Either this president doesn't have any idea what is going on around him or he figures s**t flows downhill and others can take the blame. I would rather it be the latter than the former. If the President is unaware of what is happening around him, we could be in a lot of trouble.

The fact is, both scenarios are problematic. One is just far more problematic than the other. We never want a president unaware of the happenings around him because that would mean his underlings would be running the show. Some would argue that we saw that with Reagan because he was not only a great communicator he was also great at delegating. Reagan's delegating did result in a few problems but what Presidency doesn't have a few scandals? If they are containable scandals and don't hurt the nation it is better than a scandal that would bring harm to us. The bottom line is we can't afford the problem of the President not knowing what is going on in his Administration. The second problem of the s**t flowing downhill is what probably is the case. How much that hurts the nation is debatable. It certainly goes to the credibility issue. All people make mistakes including world leaders. If the President takes the blame and follows up with a solution to the problem, people are more inclined to respect him than chastise him. If problems happen all the time and the President shoulders the blame we have to question why problems happen all the time whether he takes blame or not. It then becomes a leadership issue.

If the President insists on passing the buck it will "appear" at some point the President really doesn't know or care what is going on.

NO, YOU ARE NOT IN CONTROL OF YOUR LIFE

Contrary to what we are told by the "positive thinking" gurus, we are not in control of our lives. By that I mean we are not in control of our entire life but only control certain small parts of it. If you were to sit down and really think it out you would realize the stake others have established in your life and how it results in varying degrees of control. From the Federal government to Google to the Military to your employer to big business you have willingly, or unwillingly in some cases, ceded control of your daily existence. And unless you are someone who prefers that others dictate your every move, than it can't be a good thing. This process has been like a slow moving train in that it started long ago and doesn't seem like it will ever end. Now the entities who have gained control know this and have done it this way on purpose. Whether you call it diversionary, influential, mind control, physical coercion or all the above, it worked. As a matter of fact, it occurred while I wrote this article and it is happening right now as you read it. And the perp happens to be me! With this article I am trying to convince you that what I am saying, and in the end asking you to do, is the right thing. Now all the naysayers out there will say we have free will, a favorite of those who adhere to a religion, and therefore charge that it is all done willingly. Especially in America, the land of the free and the home of the brave. But for those of us who love America deeply, as I do, we say bull s**t. Lest we forget, the Founding Fathers warned us about this.

Let's just take a typical day in the life of a “normal” American. Normal meaning those who work for a living and obey the law. This precludes crackheads, thugs and those in the banking industry. I include the banking industry because it is 2014 and we all know now that they have been officially declared as part of the criminal element. But I digress, let's return to a typical day in the life of...you possibly? Bear in mind I am only going to point out the obvious because I am not a conspiracy theorist although these guys are starting to appear as quite normal.

On a weekday you will rise at a designated time. That time will be determined by an employer who has decided, through no evidentiary procedure, that it is the best time. You will prepare your children for school because the school district has determined their start time as well, again there is no apparent evidentiary procedure involved. Maybe they collude with the employers? You will drop your kids, still not fully awake, at their school and go on to work. Some mornings neither of you will have breakfast or time to talk because there is no time. So the grumpy kids meander into the classroom only to be confronted by an even grumpier teacher. Good start to the day, right? Meanwhile you sit in the traffic gridlock because so many employers have decided on the same start times. Now if the employer and the school used even a rudimentary evidentiary procedure they would determine that in order for the employer and the student to operate at optimum levels of productivity, creativity, and most of all, emotional engagement they would have the employee and student "ease" into the day rather than be forced by some archaic ways of doing things just because "that's the way its always been done."

And let us not forget, while on the way to work you have to fill up the tank with gas that is costing you an unbelievable amount per gallon because some 1%er doesn't seem to have enough millions. He, and I say he because it is a boys' club, will use the excuse that someone farted in Bangladesh and therefore they had no recourse but to raise the price of gas. By the way, I view the manipulation of the oil markets as the ultimate control, coming in a close second is government surveillance.

Now we are settled into work and school. At school your child will follow a curriculum determined, in all probability by the teacher's political leanings, that ranks America last in education among industrialized nations. They will follow a program that all the children will follow because teachers have determined that it is a numbers game. The powerful teachers union will always complain that the problem with education in America is the number of students in a class. This has always been, and will always be, the "reason" why some teachers do a crappy job or student academic scores are woefully low or why it rained last Tuesday. But no problem, the teachers union has found the solution! Give the teachers more money and more days off and by the way don't even think about grading a teachers performance. They insist only the kids be graded (many teachers also grade the parents) but not the teachers. Are you starting to see the control here? Looking at it just a couple of hours into the day, which part of the day have you controlled?

As we approach mid-day the employee and student will be allowed to eat at a designated time. No matter that blood sugar levels are all over the map because this is different with each individual, you will all eat at the same time. So if we were to look at the workplace and school environment as a team effort we would find wildly varying degrees of contribution based on energy levels which are determined by amounts of sleep and nutrition. It's like when I was in Little League and the coach would put little Johnny in right field as a way to keep him out of the mix because he didn't have the same level of talent. In America we are all about winning. To argue that would make you a dinosaur. But when we send a team to the Olympics we send only the best in each category. So if a coach in Little League is so obsessed with winning that he doesn't have time to develop the skills of little Johnny he just sticks him in right field (this is not an attempt to trash right fielders but rather a way to make a point) then Johnny becomes the victim because it is....out of his control.

Okay, so we are just about done with lunch. Some eaters came to the time almost depleted of energy while others were not even hungry. But hey, it's impossible to jockey the times people eat, right? So an hour after lunch people will be falling asleep because they were so hungry they overloaded at lunch and others are famished because they weren't hungry at the designated lunch hour. In all fairness I have heard about new age tech companies that refuse to follow the traditional way of doing things (for whatever reason, they found it doesn't work) and by the look of the stock market they are doing rather well. Unfortunately, for most workers and students the traditionalists have decided the new age employers are whack jobs so today's workers and students won't see any of these current methods come into play for them. Factories seem to refuse to depart from their centuries old model of doing things and in education the traditionalists view online education providers (which allows for much flexibility) as anarchists.

We are only minutes beyond the lunch hour and you can see how others are controlling your every move. Remember, at the outset I cautioned you that I am only pointing out the most obvious and direct controls. And only a few of them at that. Each of the most obvious and direct controls have a greater number of sub-set controls but I would have a serious case of writers cramp if I enumerated them all.

Just to hurry this along, because you need to get to other things that are in the control of others, you will have to return home. And you will have to hurry despite the gridlock because you have been told to pick up your children at a certain time. Don't forget the teachers have to get home to continue their work on their own time with supplies they purchased with their own money (another reason they should get shorter hours and more money, right?).

So now we are at home preparing a meal the First Lady has told us we should not be eating. In all probability we are eating what we can afford because the amount of taxes (the amount others control i.e. politicians) we pay is so much we have little left over. At least we can rest easy knowing a crackhead somewhere is getting a very delicious, free meal at our expense. I don't know about you but that helps me sleep at night. Oh, and I apologize to the fat cat because another few dollars of interest he earned on his millions is now going to an increased tax rate. God forbid he may have to wait a couple of extra minutes before he buys that new Lamborghini. Wait, I know, he can make a call to some poor schmuck in Bangladesh and ask him to cut the cheese so the price of a barrel of crude jumps. I should apologize to all farters in Bangladesh because I callously use their existence as an excuse. But really who cares about a country that works children to the bone, or death, in factories making clothes for wealthy fashion designers and corrupt corporations. The fact is the 1%ers don't really put any effort into their excuses for ripping us off. They don't have to if they have both political parties in their pockets because who is here to defend us? So to say the price for a gallon of gas is $4.15 because some worker came back from lunch late at a oil refinery in a place not a single person has ever heard of well...we all know it is bull s**t. Just accept it and go on with life because...it is out of your control.

Okay, the parents have fed the kids some God awful meal and want to take in a movie as a way to unwind. They call Alice the 14 year old next door who will babysit but only if she gets a living wage and can put her headphones on and ignore the kids. She knows she can ask for a living wage because every Democrat in Congress (and more than a few pseudo Republicans) fight for her to get that living wage. You acquiesce because you will be late for the movie due to the gridlock still on the roads. You need time also to peruse the menu of movies by way of their ratings. The government likes to control what you view by rating everything. Aren't we all better off if guys like Michael Bloomberg and Anthony Weiner decide what is good for us? So you pick an R rating because the kids are home and it is a night for the adults. Unfortunately, you sit down and realize the nimrod in front of you has brought his 6 kids raging in age from 5 to 11. So much for enforcement of the rating system. But give our politicians a break. They worked years hammering out the deal for a rating system. They had to endure many nights of being wined and dined by lobbyists. They had to take exotic excursions to islands with white sand beaches and unlimited Pina Coladas so they could see how that country's rating system works. And let's not forget, they had to have legislation of some sort they could use to hide a bridge to nowhere.

Again, I digress (I do that because I am a digressor). The happy parents are now on their way after spending half their 401K on popcorn and soda and watching sex scenes with the nimrod's children sitting in the seats in front of them. While driving (and obeying all the laws designed to control traffic) other people are flying by at never before heard of speeds and running red lights and driving drunk but they will get away scott free (sorry Scott) because the control isn't enforced.

So you may be asking yourself at this point if we are forced to submit to these controls, and you are because politicians have created laws that state you will obey them or else, why aren't they doing some good? Well, they weren't designed to be good they were designed to control. And the reasons are discretionary. Every entity is convinced they have to protect their territory. Whether it is the Government, the Military (you probably thought the Government controlled the military but they only control the funding...step on any military base and you will find it similar to the Vatican state), major corporations, the banking industry, and of course the teachers union, they all are fiercely protective. Unfortunately, those of us that are essentially the beasts of burden for these entities don't have the power they have to protect our territory. Therefore, we our placed, and kept, under their control. So anyway, they get home to find their kids have survived the babysitter and you rest your weary souls only to wake again in the morning and start the whole process over again.

So after all this dribble what am I actually saying? I guess what I am saying is the positive thinking gurus are half right. You can't control your entire life as they preach you can but you can control "parts" of your life. Don't mistake what I am saying as complete control of "parts" of your life because the sad truth is that the aforementioned entities have secured pervasive control but kindly throw us a bone in the sense they will allow us to have "some" permittable controls. As to what those controls are is anyone's guess.

THIS IS JUST STUPID

It is 2013. It happened again today. A one year old baby in a stroller was killed by gunshot on a New York street. Another tragedy stacked on top of another tragedy stacked on top of another tragedy and it goes on and on and on. By any measurement in any part of the world this should be considered horrendous. But it happened in America and America is better than this. Every spokesperson for every cause will step up and whatever their cause, will blame what happened to this child for every ill that exists in life. We are becoming a nation of talkers. Billionaire politicians will insist all the guns be taken. Pastors will insist it is embedded in our race problem. Others will cry we have become a lawless nation and we simply need to lock up more people.

What we have become is a stupid nation. We have become a greedy nation. We have become a self-absorbed nation. The well-known who will step up and speak to the people through whatever medium provides them a platform, will get the requisite attention and payday. But at the end of this horrible day we will accomplish nothing. We will continue to argue and not resolve our differences. This will morph into a hatred for each other and the problems will persist. It doesn't matter that we have an Administration and Congress that collectively possesses the greatest amount of intellect known to mankind. It doesn't matter that we are home to the greatest number of millionaires and billionaires that ever existed. It doesn't matter that our middle class numbers in the millions. At the end of this horrible day we will accomplish nothing. The groups mentioned above, when in the safety of their homes, somehow think this kind of thing will never find its way to their doorstep. That's stupid. It will come to them. At some point in time, it will come to them. Something needs to be done. If the aforementioned won't do something then they need to get out of the freaking way. While they are still pushing for that attention and almighty buck (as if they could ever get enough) they are getting in the way of somebody, somewhere that will get it done.

The bottom line is we are a nation of people talking smack. All talk and no action. We are ready to run all over the world and fix everybody elses's problems no matter the cost in lives and money. We call this protecting our “national interests” abroad. What about our interests right here at home? America will always be the biggest and baddest. We don't have to get into everybody's business every day to maintain this position. We are America! Everybody wants to live here or wants what we have. If they can't do either of those then they just hate us. If they hate us they burn American flags and then kill each other. We can't stop this. Those countries have their own whack jobs. We need to deal with our whack jobs. We need to fix our problems and not the problems of others.

Why don't we try this. We tell the oil companies to take a break from making gargantuan sums of profit for about a month. They take the politicians they have in their pockets on yet another "junket" but this time they go for the entire month. Now this vacation has to be spent in Detroit. That way they will see these problems as if they were on their doorstep. And I should add they should take a few "talking heads" with them. After all, they will need someone to attend to their luggage.

Every president that occupies the White House typically polls out at about 50% except when we drop a bomb somewhere and the poll spikes for about 20 minutes. Congress polls at about minus 3 on a good day. What's wrong with this picture? These days there is no "aisle" in Congress because you can't tell the forest for the trees.

They create legislation to fix problems but it is so heavily laden with pork it needs a Nutrisystem program. We don't need a bridge to nowhere in Alaska to fix our immigration problems at the southern border (do any Hispanics even live in Alaska?). That's just stupid. The politicians and fat cats (that may be redundant) who run this country are going to ruin this country. If a politician with a Harvard degree and a fat cat with billions want to run this country I have no problem with that. Someone has to run the show. I just want them to get their heads out of their a***s and do it right. Do it in a way that benefits everyone. Remember, politicians are elected with our votes and rich people make money when we buy their products. What happened to the concept of one hand washes the other or I will scratch your back if you will scratch mine.

I am not rich and I am not a politician so I need these guys in my life. So does everyone. We just don't need them in our lives behaving the way they are behaving. We also know that the achievements by these people are well earned and well deserved (in most cases) and they should not be denied their just rewards. The operative word here is “just”. If a person works a gazillion hours to build a business or someone goes to a great college and works a gazillion hours for an advanced degree they should be rewarded. And there is no nation better at rewarding their people than America. What I am saying is that we are in a partnership with the rich and powerful and we deserve more than a bone thrown to us. So adjust the high level of arrogance you guys all seem to possess down to a more manageable level and perhaps you will remember how we helped you get where you are. Our own President Obama famously said wherever you are in your life someone helped you get there. Remember that Prez?

So cut down the number of cocktail parties and golf outings and get down to business fixing America's problems. Once you get our problems under control feel free to help others. After all, we are a helping nation. That is one of the things that makes us strong. But right now we are in the “Houston, we've got a problem” mode. So get America back to earth instead of getting into the world's business every minute of the freaking day. In fact, you can use Detroit as a starting point. For you politicians and fat cats who have no idea where Detroit is because you are so out of touch, a basic GPS will guide you there. Or, just ask an average American because they probably know better than you.

The bad things that are happening in our great nation right now are just stupid. By that I mean they shouldn't have happened because we are smarter than that. If you are placed in charge of people or the welfare of people then you need to take that responsibility seriously. It is fine if you present a bill for what you do if what you do helps others. But if you produce a shoddy product or service you don't deserve squat. So those of you that know you are producing a shoddy product or service you need to get the hell out of the way and let the big dog take over.

IT AIN'T ABOUT YOU LARRY FLYNT

Larry Flynt and his bleeding heart doesn't want the man who shot and crippled him to be executed. The problem is, he isn't being executed for shooting you, he is being executed because he is a monster that preyed on and murdered eight people. He was convicted of those murders and is implicated in thirteen more. He murdered these people because they did not share his White Supremacist philosophy.

Joseph Paul Franklin should die. Mr. Flynt uses the standard argument employed by those who oppose the death penalty and that is that it is no deterrent. But for those of us who believe deterrence is only a component of the issue know that the other components may in fact be of greater significance. Perhaps Mr. Flynt isn't aware of prison gangs. Do you think maybe the white prison gangs have embraced Franklin and tried, or possibly succeeded, in having him kill those he hates while in prison? Maybe Franklin has disciples outside, the Charles Manson version, and is having them fulfill his hate agenda. What about the families of the victim? If some of them fell on hard times because of the loss of their loved one do you think they feel good about Franklin never having to worry about how he is going to acquire food and shelter? The State takes care of that monster's every need. Food, shelter, health care to name a few. And Larry you should be happy he has access to all the sex, drugs, and rock and roll his heart desires. And what about all the taxpayers dollars that have supported his years of appeals? That money would have been better spent going to the families of the victims. And really Larry, are you so naive that you believe any inmate in America's prisons suffer? Criminals have not only accepted the fact that imprisonment goes with the territory, they have found ways to prosper while locked up. You don't have to believe me, this stuff is documented. Do your research.

Larry, you say you would love to be in a room with him for an hour so you can inflict the same kind of damage to him as he did to you. So even if you are opposed to the death penalty, you are not opposed to shooting and crippling him apparently. Well, I'm okay with that. That would probably curtail his ability to kill while in prison or have man on man sex. I think, realistically, if he were to spend an hour in a room with you that you would talk him to death. Sometimes when I listen to you I feel like I want to die because people like you exist.

Larry, you speak of justice versus vengeance. You don't believe America should be in the business of killing people itself. Well then maybe your time would be better spent railing against Washington and the Military Industrial Complex that puts our young men and women into harm's way. After all, they are not murderers but we send them to their death anyway at the hands of rogue nations.

And Larry please, it's not as if you have not dirtied your hands. Do you suppose just maybe the career path you chose may have affected people in an adverse way? Do you think, possibly, that your business endeavors may have caused a negative impact in some circles of society? I really have to doubt your credibility among the majority of the citizenry.

You have made it a point to buck the system and have even made quite a good living from doing so. But maybe you should stop and think that there are a lot of us out here that at least like some parts of that system you buck and wish you would do your business elsewhere. Larry, you do not speak for those who lost their loved ones at the hands of this monster and you certainly don't speak for the majority of Americans who do not oppose the death penalty. You have a soapbox purchased by the proceeds of your smut factory which you have every right to use and you know it. You have been down that road before. But just like so many other celebrities who believe their fame and wealth also somehow miraculously implanted in them a unique insight into well, everything I guess, your rantings will be dismissed with a simple waving of a hand like swatting away a fly that refuses to stop bothering you.

THE SMART THING TO DO?

President Obama was in San Francisco, I am sure he fit right in, giving a speech about immigration reform in a largely immigrant Chinese community. During that speech he was being heckled by an illegal immigrant who attends UC Berkeley about how he should use Executive Order to implement immigration reform rather than trying to get Congress to agree. The student's name is Ju Hong. This is wrong on so many levels.

The President started by blaming the Republicans. Nothing ever seems to be the fault of this president. He is the Teflon president. He said immigration reform is up to the Republicans. No, it is up to the people and if the people are telling the Republicans we don't want it then it is us holding it up, Mr. President. Do you want to blame us instead? The President's response was to a heckler. Free speech is great but decorum in certain situations must be followed. Heckling our President is kinda rude. I am obviously not a big fan of the president (although I voted for him but ended up unhappy with his policies) but I am less of a fan of people heckling my president. And to add insult to injury it was an illegal immigrant.

I'm going to presume (at the risk of giving a liberal a heart attack) he is of Chinese descent based on the name and the neighborhood. Aren't I the profiler. So anyway, this guy is imploring the president to invoke executive order. Isn't that why the Chinese want to get out of their country because everything is by executive order? But it is usually the case that immigrants come to America for our way of life but rather than assimilate they instead want us to be more like their country. Well...then why are they here? To add even more insult to more injury the president said he would do it if he could. What does that say about our president? That he is the socialist people accuse him of being?

Everybody wants immigration reform. Whether it is the crowd that wants the military on the border or the crowd that wants to give carte blanche to the illegals they all agree we need reform. But it has to be by the will of the people not by executive order. The president refers to the "harder process" which is the democratic process. Really Mr. President? Is it so hard that you just go the way of the dictator and say it is your way or the highway? You are lending credence to the assertion you are a socialist.

The president speaks of talented young college graduates leaving to go to other nations to ply their trade. What's wrong with that? We can't employ are own college graduates or haven't you heard? Are you kidding me? We offer up our educational system to illegal immigrants (and I'm sure we end up paying most of the tab) and when they graduate you're worried about whether or not they can find a job when your own people can't? Unbelievable.

And you say by keeping these people here it would cut the deficit and add a trillion dollars to the economy. Where do you get these numbers? Do you get them on the fly or did you actually leave the office this morning with carefully prepared stats from your Harvard educated staff? If we can't employ our own people to do this, how would we do it with illegal immigrants. The president ends his speech by saying “This isn’t just the right thing to do,” he said “It’s the smart thing to do.” How is it smart and how is it right? What is smart and right is to have the American people agree on a compromise that makes both sides happy. It's a no-brainer. It seems to me that the only people the president is listening to is the illegal immigrants. I question how much input they should have. If we were in their country would their elected officials listen to us? I think not.

I have an idea. Why don't we adopt Mexico's or China's immigration policy?

SO MUCH FOR BEING BEST BUDS

Apparently, the financial ties we have with China certainly don't bind because the events today in the East China Sea highlight the tensions between China and pretty much everyone else. China has been locked in a dispute with Japan over a grouping of islands each claim as their own. In recent days China used a "pull it out of your a*s" move by claiming the airspace over the islands as their own. China, being the bully in that region, put out a warning that anyone violating this new airspace will be dealt with militarily. So of course our brilliant military tacticians decided to test that theory. Oh, that's smart.

Now China has known for the longest time that Japan, South Korea, and the United States would be conducting war games in the area. So their timing is certainly suspect. Even though all powerful nations conduct war games they always do it in a way that it offends another powerful nation. It's like little boys calling each other out to fight on the playground. But all it really does is show how it doesn't matter how rich or smart or powerful a country's leadership is, they still do STUPID s**t. Meanwhile, the citizens in these countries are sitting in their living rooms watching this crap unfold in the media.

How do you explain to your citizenry that you are going do things to bring your nation to the brink of war? You don't. That is the state of things today. It's politicians

gone wild. You act in a way that is difficult to explain and you do it regardless of what the people of your nation think. The Administration should not condone the beating of the chest when we are in someone else's neighborhood because they are going to view it as us f**king with them. What would be the point of that?

By getting into everybody's affairs the United States spreads itself too thin. It's like America having ADD. If your focus is spread out too much then those areas that may require more focus than the others are going to suffer. In the end it is always the American people who pay the price. So if we are thousands of miles away playing war games with friends we are taking our eye off the ball somewhere else. And if we add to that doing STUPID s**t like possibly provoking a nation that thinks they are more powerful than they actually are, we could find ourselves in an incredible mess.

Quit acting like little boys!

AND NOW THIS

Today's news from Mexico actually comes from the UN Nuclear Agency and it isn't good. A truck has been stolen in Mexico that has a shipment of radioactive material that can be used to create a “dirty bomb.” The likelihood of a rogue terrorist cell getting their hands on a dirty bomb is far more probable than a rouge nation getting their hands on a nuclear weapon. It is like the thug in the hood getting a Saturday night special versus a new Glock. It would probably be a low level thug short on cash so he will take whatever is available to him. Likewise with the rouge terrorist cell not operating under the umbrella of a more sophisticated terrorist organization.

The incident in Mexico could unfold in a number of different ways. If you have ever been to the country you know that Mexico has a wildly divergent cross section of peoples. It is evident immediately upon entering the country unless you are hogtied and blindfolded in the trunk of a car. You have the Elitists, a burgeoning middle class, and the impoverished. The impoverished make up the majority of the country hence the constant flood of Mexican citizens into the United States. Those of the impoverished that cannot find their way into the States are left to fend for themselves as Mexico really doesn't have a welfare system of any note. It certainly isn't a well funded system like we have in America.

So the scenarios can go like this:

- a street thug steals a truck and sells the contents for scrap and it is handled as if it is scrap (regulation of small scrap businesses is almost non-existent in Mexico)

- the thug is more sophisticated, knows he may have something valuable, puts it out for bid

- a Middle Eastern terrorist on his way to America through Mexico or an American terrorist hi-jacked the cargo knowing what it is and plans to build a bomb

- a cartel steals the cargo knowing what it is and peddles it to terrorist groups for a high dollar amount because they know its value

- a rouge authority in search of the material finds it and decides to sell it to the highest bidder

I can go on all day with scenarios like this but I'm sure you get the point. My home town borders Mexico and my wife grew up in Mexico so these scenarios are very real to me and very frightening. The media in its infinite wisdom and in their unrelenting search for "the truth" was kind enough to give out so many details that every person of ill repute and/or any financially desperate individual is now scrambling to find this truck. It is tantamount to giving away the military's battle plan to the enemy. But a reporter's quest for recognition is going to override any shred of sensible action that may keep a lid on the situation.

So if you are not scared sh*tless by now then now would be a good time.

PROTECTING OUR PRESIDENT

The event regarding the fake interpreter at the Mandela memorial service speaks volumes about how we protect our President. Or is it a statement about how we don't protect our President. Given that we have discovered recent indiscretions by the United States Secret Service it is probably not surprising that this fake interpreter found himself standing right next to our President. And then to make matters a whole lot worse the guy admits to be schizophrenic and violent. It eventually came out that he has an extensive record of serious crimes and was once arrested for murder. This is so over the top it is hard to even comprehend.

It's difficult to understand why a host country like South Africa would put so many world leaders at risk. That's just stupid. How the f**k they run that country is beyond me. With all the volatility in that part of the world it is mind boggling that they would not employ the very highest levels of security. If a guy like this knucklehead is able to do what he did I guess we should thank our lucky stars that nothing tragic occurred.

But despite the South African Keystone Cops version of protection, where the hell was our Secret Service? Drinking and chasing hookers? Seriously. Where were those guys? If South African personnel have a brain fart our guys should be there to say, what the f**k are you doing? Right? Do we go to countries in that volatile region and not monitor how they handle security for our guy? Our guy happens to be the most powerful leader in the free world and we don't ensure his safety?

There has been enough serious revelations about the Secret Service that an investigation has to be undertaken. The fact they were not aware of South Africa's near tragic, inexcusable mistake should provide the impetus for the investigation. If I were the president I would be pissed and initiating that investigation myself.

I am not a big fan of the current president but he is still my president and I don't want him in harm's way. Our people should be the back up in every situation so if the host country does not do its job properly we step in and correct the situation or we take our guy back home. Our president should never be put at risk and if he is then heads need to roll.

This entire debacle is unacceptable.

OBAMA'S NOT WORRIED

Most presidents in their last term are so concerned with their legacy to the point they will make decisions driven by by that concern. Apparently, this is not the case with Obama. He believes, and it's hard to dispute, that his core group is strong enough and large enough that his legacy will be accepted just as he has engineered it. This is the same core group that never flinched when Bill Clinton got a blow job in the White House.

Thanks in large part to the Republican Party alienating voters, young people that don't have a political clue, and all the illegal voters this core group has taken on a momentum that will turn the entire country into what California already is, a liberal bastion. So all the wackiness you see on a daily basis in California is what you will see nationwide. Even a crackhead could see this coming.

So Obama can wallow in the morass of low poll ratings and not fear any damage to his legacy. Especially when that legacy will be written almost entirely by same thinking scholars. What happened is an aide came into Obama's office one day to discuss the President's plummeting poll numbers and was told by the prez, no worries. He explained to the aide that if Congress can have a single digit poll rating and continue to get reelected, he (meaning Obama) isn't too worried. Obama explained how his decision to become the country's ATM would overide any disillusion anyone may feel about his perfomance. By using the Federal Reserve to create money he has befriended a banking industry who otherwise would not like him and he has befriended the downtrodden by extending unemployment insurance a gozillion times and making sure every third person is getting food stamps.

So in the future when the Republican Party no longer exists (has that already happened?) our grandkids will pick up a history book, written by a liberal, and read a glowing legacy of a man who nearly bankrupted the nation.

CHARLIE'S RANTING AGAIN!

Charlie Sheen, in his latest twitter rant, must have had a dictionary handy because he was using words no recent high school grad should be using. Yes, Charlie just graduated high school this year. Don't you love it when you see this kind of enthusiasm in our senior citizens (I know, Charlie's not a senior but he certainly looks like one because of all the abuse to his body).

Anyway, Charlie is ripping Paul Robertson the star of Duck Dynasty for his comments on homosexuality. Charlie, being the good socialist (it's in the genes his father is Martin Sheen) doesn't believe in free speech for anyone but himself. Part of Charlie's fame is that he has a constant mouth full of poop. Charlie rips Phil using multi-syllable words which he has no business using. Charlie also continues with his usually incoherent stringing together of phrases hoping to coin something for the sake of posterity. But one phrase he used did make me laugh. He called Phil a "shower dodger." We may actually hear that one a hundred years from now. And what is Charlie's problem with mallards? In a game of checkers with Charlie, a mallard would probably win.

Charlie, you are known primarily for your comedic talents and social shortcomings not your intellect. Even with that dictionary you probably shouldn't engage in an intellectual battle with anyone other than a crackhead or a fifth grader (I apologize to fifth graders everywhere).

The irony in all of this completely floors me. Of all the people to critize hurtful comments spoken by someone about another we have the king of hurtful comments, Charlie Sheen. I mean really. And the Daily News, among others, gives this guy recognition? Maybe it was meant in jest because it was so ridiculous. Usually, when you present a response to something somebody said that could be labeled as truly offensive you would be wise to choose someone above reproach. Quoting Charlie Sheen is like quoting Al Sharpton. Neither of them would know credibilty if it bit them in the butt.

And Charlie, what is this crap about you wanting to stick up for your friends that might be offended? How many "minutes" has it been since you uttered your last gay slur. You are the master of hypocrisy. You use offensive speech to critsize offensive speech . Go figure. And two things Charlie, Phil was wealthy by way of "dirt-clod stacking" long before he had a television show and it is more admirable to earn a television show by accomplishing something than to find your way into Hollywood by being the son of Martin Sheen. If it weren't for your dad you would be a standard issue crackhead living in a gutter somewhere. And the remark about Phil being a "surviving brain donor", at least he has a brain to donate. Remember, you just finished high school.

I don't have a single gay friend and I would prefer they not cook in my kitchen but that doesn't mean I accept people trashing them for the way they live. To each his own. No harm, no foul.

And I will remind you Charlie you lost a television series because of the poop coming from your mouth and you have yet to land a new one. I stand corrected I was just informed you do have a new show, I will try to get the word out for you.

THE WORD POLICE

An article this morning by Jamie P. Chandler, a political scientist at Hunter College and The Colin L. Powell School for Civic and Global Leadership at City College of New York piqued my interest. It was a dig at what he claims is Monica Crowley's "exceptional imagination" when she claimed A & E's response to the Phil Robertson incident was because of pressure from the "word police." Mr. Chandler claimed it was not political correctness but rather bad judgement that spurred the event. He believes there is no such thing as word police.

Those remarks are a testament to Mr. Chandler's exceptional naivete because there is such a thing as the "word police." Although we experience it more in a metaphorical sense, we do have laws on the books today that are relatively new that govern our speech. And let us not forget there is a liberal around every corner ready to tell us what is right or wrong with our speech. Based on the comments he received I believe Mr. Chandler stepped in the proverbial pile of poop. And in his answers to the comments he comes off as the "word police" Monica Crowley was speaking of. His answers were more like instructions on how we, and especially Phil, should answer questions like the ones posed by the GQ reporter.

What is more disturbing is the fact that this kind of

discussion gets so much air time. While all you freakin' liberals and conservatives were getting your panties in a bunch people were being murdered, children molested, and unjust wars continued. But you feel your time is better spent bitching about what someone says that might hurt your precious feelings. From Jamie Chandler to Monica Crowley to Sarah Palin to Charlie Sheen I say keep your eye on the ball and focus on susbstantive issues. This is America we don't need to have a discussion about free speech because it is our freakin' right and I got a kid in the Marines who is willing to die for that right.

Every time you guys get an opportunity to position yourself to be heard it is simply an exercise in boosting your ego. Nothing changes as a result of these discussions except your pay check and your recognition. But if you are happy to gain your riches by wasting everyone's time talking about these frivilous issues there is nothing I can do because it also is your right to waste oxygen. To make an issue of free speech in a free America is absurd. Too many lives have been sacrificed so idiots like Phil Robertson can say the crap he says. He has the right. So if some gay guy doesn't like it is that same gay guy going to go to war and take a bullet for the preservation of our freedoms? I don't think so. Because if he did he would shut his pie hole knowing that free speech means just that, free speech! You may not like it but too bad, this is the Land of the Free and the Home of the Brave. I don't believe in man on man sex but if that's what you want to do you are free to do it. But I am also free to say I don't think you should. But that very statement will have people coming out of the woodwork (and some will even threaten me with death) to tell me I have no right to say that in public. Mr. Chandler, those people are "word police" and they are everywhere. They are not sanctioned by our government (or are they?) or backed by a union. You won't find positions offered in the help wanted section for the word police. They are self-employed freelancers. This group is almost entirely made up of liberals with possibly a few misguided conservatives. Their intent is to manage our lives. It goes way beyond policing what we say. They want to manage what we feel.

I am a registered Independent because my political thoughts are varied. If I belonged to the Democratic Party or the Republican Party they wouldn't be. My thoughts would be their thoughts. I am agnostic so my thoughts are not regulated by any particular religious group. I like this arrangement in my life because it allows me more choice. I do have a steadfast belief in our Constitution and our republic. I also believe the caretakers of that are doing a horrible job and I don't know how they sleep at night. Because the practice of stereotyping rules the day among all groups in America I will say I am a white guy born in the mid-west. The word police will want to know that in case they are preparing an attack plan.

Mr. Chandler's naivete aside, I think the bigger problem

is the double standard employed by the word police. One of it's members, Charlie Sheen, came out of his den of porn almost immediately to condemn Robertson's remarks. Wasn't it just a few weeks ago that Mr. Sheen was demonizing gays? And I understand he is not a big fan of Jewish people either. And if you are monogamous you might want to steer clear of Charlie.

Hollywood types are freelancing word police who routinely don't practice what they preach. Charlie is just one of many. They typically defer to their craft when they are forced to defend a double standard. Much of what they do is part of the art form, as they say. They have creative license to talk out of both sides of their mouth. And of course the intellectual elite, of which I am sure Mr. Chandler includes himself, feel they are above it all and are always ready to school the rest of us dumb-asses.

If you have a platform by virtue of being a Hollywood star or a really smart person or a person with great wealth you should use it responsibly for the good of all people and not just for those who share your political leanings. Instead these platforms are used to advance far left or far right thinking that devolves into contentious discussions that really don't help anyone. The ones who risked and lost their lives for us to have free speech had no idea the future would bring us political correctness and too sensitive feelings. By the way, I have never watched an episode of Duck Dynasty.

TALK IS CHEAP

The liberals insistence on talking sense to our enemies is backfiring once again but in a very big way. Iran's announcement today of the development of equipment designed to enhance the enrichment of uranium is yet another attempt to bone us. These rag-tag, pseudo warriors live to make America look foolish and Obama, the liberals reigning representative, is doing his best to help them. I have to agree with Israel (and now Saudi Arabia?) that Iran has no intention of veering off its path to the creation of a nuclear warhead. What they are doing now is duping Obama into releasing monies the United States is holding and the Iranians need, badly.

In pursuing this already doomed diplomacy Obama is risking alienating allies that are extremely important to us in that region. Most importantly Israel and Saudi Arabia. There is no better authority on the motivations of Iran than Israel. Iran is Israel’s most dangerous enemy and they are in the neighborhood. Can you imagine Israel's frustration as they watch what is going on in the negotiations between the United States and Iran? Can you imagine the helplessness they feel because of

Obama's treatment of Israel as an afterthought. Obama's "step aside we'll take care of this" attitude puts Israel in a most precarious position. Iran has been steadfast regarding two important points. They have never backed down from their assertion that no other country will be allowed to cross Iran's "red line" and force them to dismantle their nuclear facilities they claim are for peaceful purposes. And secondly, they have never renounced their declaration that Israel should be wiped from the earth.

Iran's willingness to engage in these talks tells us that the sanctions are working. In that region countries are erupting in violence because they are tired of their current way of life. Iran knows that it is just a matter of time and that sentiment will manifest itself in their country. As a preemptive measure they need to appease their people and one way to do that is to get their hands on confiscated monies that belong to them and contracts for oil which will provide a revenue stream. They have skillfully created a bargaining chip with their nuclear ambitions which could be about as real as the weapons of mass destruction that provided a pretense for the war in Iraq. They predicted the giddiness of the Obama Administration when they signaled they were willing to enter into talks. Now they are close to getting what they want because Obama hasn't hid the fact he is chomping at the bit to ease the sanctions despite the absence of any real evidence that Iran will comply with anything.

Israel is desperately trying to warn us and now Saudi Arabia is questioning Obama's handling of foreign policy especially in light of the “red line” fiasco in Syria. Even fellow democrats are unsure about the easing of the sanctions. As long as Iran is sending conflicting messages and because we know their history we should not be gifting them with the easing of sanctions. If we ease sanctions the difficulty in reasserting them will be monumental.

And meanwhile they are still creating centrifuges.

THE REPUBLICANS JUST DON'T GET IT

This statement in an article from foxnews.com says it all;

"Major Sunni tribes turned against Al Qaeda before the American withdrawal at the end of 2011. But they do not support the Shiite-led government in Iraq, creating an odd alliance in the battle against militants."

In the same article Senators McCain and Graham chastise President Obama for today's takeover of Fallujah by Al Qaeda forces. The statement above is telling because it gives the reader a truncated glimpse into how convoluted the situation is in that part of the world, not just Iraq. There are simply too many players and the motivations are also many as well as varied.

We were in Vietnam because of a communist threat. Today we live in a world full of communists and America is doing just fine. We are in the Middle East because of a terrorist threat (or so "they" say) and if we leave we will be fine. What the Republicans refuse to admit is we are losing lives and spending money in an area and in a way that isn't working. When you don't get the outcome you want you have to change your approach. If you keep doing the same thing that didn't work before and hope you will succeed you are a fool. The Republicans are fools. I know. I was once a Republican. I now happily vote as an

Independent.

John McCain never met a war he didn't like. He also never met a skirmish he didn't feel he could turn into a war. John McCain is a bully. And it seems he never goes anywhere without his sidekick Sen. Lindsey Graham. Are they the current version of Mutt and Jeff? That part of the world is within reach of a number of industrialized nations not to mention superpowers all of which are playing a minor role while the United States is the beast of burden. I won't ask why because we never get a straight answer let alone an honest one. I will simply say we need to get the f**k out of there and to hell with the war hawks. It is a mess we will never be able to clean up. We are not the world's police department. And regardless of the flavor of the month threat the politicians are going with we can handle things if we are not in everybody's house in the Middle East.

We best every country in the world in every significant category that matters. Of all these threats the Republicans claim we need to guard against most of them are bogus. They act as if doomsday is tomorrow. As a political party they are losing ground every day and the infighting is an embarrassment. Hillary is going to be the next President of the United States no matter what candidate the Republicans offer up. And the way the Republican Party is behaving it is only helping her to win. Bill sees it and is laughing his ass off. He will be the First Gentleman.

In berating the Republicans I am in no way endorsing Barack Obama. I believe now he is doing a terrible job and I regret voting for him. But when you offer up McCain and Romney as alternatives you literally shoot yourself in the foot. If the Democrats continue to win while being far to the left then the Republicans better think about moving toward the center but they refuse to budge from their far right position. Good luck with that one. The only time the Republicans pay attention to a poll is when it is heavily in their favor. If they were to listen to the American public instead of their wealthy donors they would know the American people want out of the mess over there. The last poll showed only 17% of Americans support our efforts in Afghanistan and they are all crackheads.

I don't like war but war happens. It has been a lot of years since we have successfully prosecuted a war and the reason for that is because the way we do it. We have too many rules and the enemy has none. I believe we should cut off the head of the snake as quickly as possible and not worry about how we do it. Who is going to criticize us? China, Russia? Who gives a crap what they think? Their governments have taken corruption to new levels. Our real friends will stand with us.

When we send our soldiers into harm's way you can call it war or a security agreement if it makes you feel better. I've got a kid in the Marines and I call it the way I see it. If they are among the enemy it is war. F**k the semantics. Obama, as much as I hate to admit it, was right to get us out of Iraq and we should leave Afghanistan this afternoon. It ain't working. A congress with an approval rating of 16% on a good day can't find their ass with both hands. Those whack jobs over there are not as dangerous as the Republicans want us to believe. When it comes right down to it, as far as the Republicans are concerned, our business over there is just that, business. As in our business interests. Worldwide the Republicans run interference for the fat cats. Even a crackhead living under a rock knows that. It is the same with the Democrats and those who use the government as a human feeding trough. The Democrats will do anything to protect that voting bloc. But the Democrats have the political advantage so whatever they are doing to gain that the Republicans better take notice.

Mid-term elections are around the corner and the Presidency is up for grabs in 2016 so if you trot out McCain and Graham to promote something that is hugely unpopular, what are you saying about your desire to win?

COMING TO AMERICA

It is 2014 and it was reported this morning that two executives were held hostage at a Goodyear plant for 30 hours by a union that isn't pleased with the fact the plant may have to close. I know, so don't lie, as you were reading this you presumed you were reading a story about an event occurring in America. Be honest. I know this because we are all aware there is a element in politics (I won't mention the name Barack Obama) that favors the European model of society that places workers in a more elevated position than they currently hold.

The story actually has to do with a plant in France (no surprise) and the tactic is one that has been in play for so long it has its own reference. It's call Boss-Napping. And just to add some punch to this French spectacle, if you recall it was only a couple of weeks ago that French President Hollande engineered a high court decision to raise the tax on anyone making over a million dollars a year to 75%.

With that in mind I ask you to direct your attention to recent events in the United States that looked at in a singular fashion may seem harmless but if looked at as a whole may appear eerily similar to certain components of the European model of the workplace and, frankly, life as they know it.

Let's begin with the idea that our current president has exhibited behaviors that one would associate with socialism. The European model of governing is socialistic. Congress is overrun by Democrats and so are the largest states in the union. Democrats behave as socialists. Democrats are supported by the unions. In America right now there is a movement, and in some locales it has already succeeded, to raise the minimum wage to what is called a living wage. Any moment now Congress, backed by the Administration, is going to extend unemployment benefits, again. The Administration has been fighting for years to get corporations and the wealthy to "carry more of the load." As the Administration has been mining for new tax revenues they have also been creating new programs and enhancing existing programs (food stamps and unemployment benefits come to mind) to spend that money.

The Obama Administration has made no secret of their desire to have government play a more invasive role in the lives of American citizens. His appointments to the Supreme Court, the unleashed Eric Holder, Obamacare, economic inequality, the circumvention of Congress as a political tactic (Chicago politics at its finest), and the shmooshing of dictators and tyrants using his lapdog John Kerry are just a few examples.

There is certainly room to improve in all these aforementioned areas but to do it in the way the

Europeans do it is wrong. Just look at the problems they have. As a nation we are the most free and the most prosperous. But even a great nation constantly needs to improve. President Obama is no dummy. He sees the Congress for what it is, impotent. So while Congress is off fighting like kids on a playground he has found a way to advance his agenda. No president, Democrat or Republican, should be left to their own devices because invariably they will shape our society in a way that benefits a specific group rather than the entire populace.

Rather than adopting a European model of governing, let's keep with the American model of governing but make it better. There is a reason why America is the greatest nation on earth, you are living it today.

WHAT IS THE POINT?

I was surprised the other day when I read Meryl Streep stole the spotlight to trash Walt Disney while presenting an award to Emma Thompson. It was kinda like Taylor Swift and Kanye West, in a way. The focus of the presentation was Emma Thompson, I thought. Did Meryl tell Emma beforehand that she was going to use the opportunity to trash Walt Disney, a man who died in 1966? Ms. Streep accused Disney of being anti-Semitic and he “didn't like women.” Quick everybody, run for the hills!

I don't know how many Disney films Meryl Streep has acted in but I bet it's more than a few. One is actually coming out now with her in it. Should we call out Ms. Streep for being a hypocrite. It least she is alive. Calling out a dead man from an entirely different era is like being a bully. He can't fight back. Is Ms. Streep a bully? And by the way, is there anyone in Hollywood, past or present, that can't be called out for something? It's not like these guys are model citizens.

People in the entertainment business live and work in a bubble. Sometimes they step out of that bubble to advance their opinion. What makes them think we want to hear their opinion? Or is it just their outsized egos at work? For a community that has little or no tolerance for people who do not think like them, how do they defend trashing others for not having tolerance? It is not just fame and fortune Hollywood royalty has achieved, they have also achieved perfection, apparently. “Do not judge, or you too will be judged” according to scripture.

I am not sure of the point Ms. Streep was hoping to make. If Mr. Disney had flaws I am not surprised. In that era many men, and women, displayed tendencies that they, hopefully, would be ashamed of today. But for the sake of argument let's say Mr. Disney did have those flaws that were exhibited by many men of that era, did he perhaps do enough good to warrant forgiveness? Or is Ms. Streep incapable of forgiveness?

WHO ARE THESE PEOPLE?

The media (all of the media) believe there is an audience for some of the pure, unadulterated crap they serve up and I would like to know who that audience is. For instance, the last few days Dennis (the worm) Rodman has been grabbing headlines for going over and kissing the ass of a guy that fed his uncle to the dogs. Why do we need to know this? It couldn't be for the shock value because no one is shocked by anything "the worm" does. And Meryl Streep gets in the news for trashing Walt Disney. For crying out loud the guy has been dead since 1966. What is her point? And why do they keep covering anything Alec Baldwin has to say? I liked him in 30 Rock but in real life the guy is a nut job. And can I get at least one day without seeing or hearing something about Kim Kardashian and Kanye West? And what about the juvenile behavior between the Fox network and every other network? Is this news? They are like kids fighting on the playground.

I have to believe the media has adopted the same position as our politicians and that is that the average American is basically a dumb-ass and grabs any little piece of information thrown to them like scraps to a dog. They must think in order to get our attention focused on the real news they have to lure us in with appetizers laced with stupidity. So exactly where does this audience come from? Politicians and the media live by polls and demographics so they must know. Is it the same group that elected President Obama? We know they weren't rocket scientists. It couldn't be anyone under 30 because they get their news from John Stewart. I know it's not the baby boomers because they don't give a crap about Kim Kardashian and Kanye West (especially Kanye).

I wouldn't be so concerned about this except for the fact it is rained down on me every single moment of every day. I remember back in the day when the National Enquirer and the Star News was being attacked incessantly by the main stream media for producing news they considered far from worthy. It was "tabloid journalism" or something to that effect. Today, you would be hard pressed to tell the difference. I just can't see a person who is acutely interested in developments regarding Iran's nuclear ambitions fast forwarding to the latest on what Kim Kardashian's ass looks like today. That disparity in thought is hard for me to imagine. That being said, there is obviously two different audiences. One for the real news and one for the fake news. What I don't get, and it scares the hell out of me, is the audience must be sizable enough for the fake news in order to get the ratings needed to get sponsors on board. That means there is enough viewers out there that care what Dennis Rodman is doing, to make it economically feasible.

ALL THINGS EQUAL, NOT!

This morning it was reported a 28 year old female teacher in Mobile County Alabama was sentenced to 6 months in prison, 5 years probation, and loss of her teaching credential. And during her probation period she won't be allowed to work with minors. The sentence was the result of a conviction for "engaging in a sexual act or deviant sexual intercourse with a student under the age of 19." The male victim in this case was 14 at the time. I'm sorry but this just makes me freakin' barf. Between the lunatic judge in Montana that sentenced a guy to 30 days for rape because the victim "wasn't blameless" because of the way she conducted herself (she was 14 and he was also a teacher) and this judge in Mobile County I'm going bonkers. They should create a show called America's Jurassic Judicial System.

This whole thing is disturbing on a number of levels. The disparity in sentencing in matters of this nature is striking especially when it comes to females having sex with minors. First of all let's call it was it is; molestation. Secondly, I have to wonder if the new model for punishment, in the matter of women, is hatched by judicial types in the back rooms of porn shops. When these judges sentence women (there have been numerous cases like the one mentioned in the opening paragraph) I wouldn't be surprised if they do it with a wink and a nod to the defendant. And when has the rights of women been so insignificant that a judge in Montana can be so brazen in placing blame on a 14 year old girl. We have always known that defense lawyers try to incriminate the victim in an effort to get their pathetic clients off the hook. And to add insult to injury these guys are usually court appointed and paid by the taxpayer they just reamed. And what does it say about our educational system that if you send your child to public school they could be in more danger than if they were walking the streets. Your child could be molested by a teacher, shot, knifed, beat up by a bully and unfortunately the list goes on.

Women and children deserve to be protected against unwanted and unprovoked assaults. If society fails in policing itself we must rely on our judicial system. If that is broken then what? Vigilantism? As a man (a real man) I am shocked at the passive approach other men take in these matters. The idea that you don't do something if it isn't in your backyard is absurd because all of America is our backyard. Why hasn't the judge in Montana been run out of town? Why don't the overseers of our judicial system overturn these ridiculously light sentences that deter nothing? We seem to be more interested in smoking pot legally and getting our hands on the latest high tech gadget or running down the latest person who used the N word. I can't say this problem is generational because many of these judges are long past their expiration dates.

And where is super cop Eric Holder in these matters. Why didn't he go to Montana and personally thump this judge? Is he afraid to go to Cheney country? And what about the Cheneys in all of this? Where were they when this went down in their neighborhood?

The blame for this debacle of justice falls on all of us. It's time to set aside the popular causes for a moment and take on some of those that garner little attention. We all have mothers, wives, daughters, sons...you get my point.

Time to man and woman up. Don't be afraid. Good and decent people will never fault you for sticking up for children or protecting defenseless women against predators.

TO ALL THE WUSSIES THAT WON'T PICK UP A GUN

I'm bone tired hearing the plaintive moans of those men who lack intestinal fortitude. This would include a wide swath of liberal thinkers. A good number of them are currently at MSNBC. This outburst of mine is a reaction to the Jack Tapper interview with Marcus Luttrell and Mark Wahlberg. When the producers contacted Mr. Luttrell about appearing for the interview I would bet my last nickel they told him it was to discuss the movie Lone Survivor. The movie is based on the book of the same name written by Luttrell who is the "lone survivor" of an operation gone wrong in Afghanistan and resulted in the loss of American warriors.

What Mr. Trapper did was use Luttrell under the pretense he was going to be interviewed about the movie to air his views on the war in Afghanistan. That's like Meryl Streep using Emma Thompson's award speech to trash Walt Disney. And what makes me sick to my stomach is that these same liberals pontificate on how proud they are of our military. Bull s**t! That's lip service at best. What these wussies need to do is interview the politicians that get us into these dumb-ass wars. Yeah, Afghanistan is a dumb-ass war but what does that have to do with a soldier doing his job with the final outcome being our safety and that of the wussies too? Marcus

Luttrell didn't start the war in Afghanistan. He was just doing his job and his book is a tribute to the men who died that day. It is a way for those of us who benefit from their willingness to guard our freedoms just what these guys go through. I admire Mark Wahlberg for not giving into the trap Tapper set. I would have liked to see Mr. Luttrell get up and clock Tapper for trying to make him out to be nothing more than an accessory to the politicians who like to start wars and send everyone else's sons and daughters to fight them.

I am a registered Independent who is conservative but I am hard pressed to believe that any war/skirmish since WWII is righteous. The politicians get us into wars, not soldiers. Most of these politicians have never served. I have a kid in the military and another set to join. I am immensely proud of them as you should be. They will fight for the rights of wussie men everywhere because it is their job. I believe when we do go to war we should go in and just obliterate the bastards and get out. But I don't believe we should have been in Iraq or Afghanistan.

Another tragic irony in all of this is the liberal wussies don't want us to get into any war, blame the soldiers, and then push for rules on the way our soldiers fight which leaves them open to be targets. The prosecution of these conflicts is more than suspect. These same wussies won't stand up to our enemies around the world or the criminal element here in America. These same guys that like to talk s**t never get "involved." If you are in trouble on the street don't expect them to help you. They are the antithesis of the real man. I laugh when I hear them trashing conservatives because they always do it from a place of safety and not a parking lot where they would get their asses kicked. It's like Alec Baldwin talking smack to a photographer. What's a photographer going to do? And Alec only does his act when he knows someone is nearby to stop things before they get too far out of hand. The law of averages dictates that one day one of these photographers is going to say hell no and punch out Baldwin. As far as I know Baldwin has no tough guy credentials. It ain't tough to trash gays and children (especially your own daughter).

So if you wussie men out there want to play tough then play tough with impotent politicians, child molesters, rapists, and gang members rather than America's brave soldiers. You make me sick Tapper.

A MILLIONAIRE'S VISION

An interesting proposition coming from a place you wouldn't expect is having people sit up and take notice. Ron Unz, a Silicon Valley multimillionaire, is pushing for an increase in the minimum wage in California to $12 an hour. Mr. Unz is a Republican. I'll wait until you get back up off the floor and in your seat. Ready? Okay, let's look at his reasoning. He claims by boosting the minimum wage we solve or mitigate multiple, serious problems in California's economic system. These are not in order of importance but let us say they are all important in and of themselves. It would push minimum wage workers closer to a living wage, lessen the dependence on food stamps among that group, increase tax revenue, make these type jobs more appealing to U.S. residents slowing the flow of illegal immigration, lessen the burden on taxpayers by decreasing the flow of tax dollars into entitlement programs, could provide the impetus to eliminating some entitlement programs drawing government away from the logic it has to be a safety net to the extent they are today.

Small business doesn’t see it quite the same way and wonder out loud how they are going to cover the increase in operating costs. In all probability consumers would realize a requisite increase in prices which would offset a good portion of those increased costs. Consumers would have an expanded array of choices because they could now shop and eat at places they would not have patronized in the past forcing businesses to compete and as a result drive that increased pricing back down.

At face value it seems like a win-win situation.

IF A CONSERVATIVE WERE TO ...

Let's say the hard to imagine happens and conservatives were to actually examine the state of the poor with it in mind that something constructive could take place without it being labeled a handout. Tough to do, huh? Well, I am a conservative but of a different stripe. That's right. We are not like bundled securities that someone tries to make look all the same. There really is variations in conservative thought but for now a certain contingent of conservatives are getting all the headlines (the political game) and overshadowing the rest of us. MSNBC and Fox only report the far left and far right viewpoints as if the more centrist of us are the red headed stepchild. I, and the other 3 people that think like me, do exist and represent a more palatable type of conservative than the raging far-right lunatic that is presented in the main stream media. Those guys actually piss me off because their antics take center stage and they promote their conservative message as the only one to the point others refuse to believe there is another kind conservatism out there.

So as a conservative who has values more aligned with a centrist approach I would say to the Old Guard and the Tea Party, “Man why don't you shut up for a minute.” And the basis for that feeling is the fact we are losing ground to the point of becoming irrelevant. For crying out loud they are building museums as we speak with wax figures of John McCain, Sean Hannity, Jim DeMint, Rush Limbaugh...you get my point. These people have good ideas but not all their ideas are good. In fact, some of their ideas are so damaging that when an election comes around it brings out the type of liberal thinker that couldn't find their ass with two hands and hasn't voted in years but does so in response to the latest salvo against the poor from the far right. To package the poor like Wall Street packaged mortgage securities is to say there is no difference in the plight of the poor because they are all the same and they are all intent on feeding at the government trough.

My father always taught me to pull myself up by my own boot straps. He said you can either be carried or you can do the carrying. In American society there will always be people who will need help and deservedly so. And there will be people who will scam the government almost as a profession. The people who need to be carried are the ones who, through some fault not of their own, have found themselves in a position that requires they ask for help. At times in my life I have been there. We should help these people. And then there are people who are helped by us who should be in jail. And we should put them there. Unfortunately our government (which includes the far-right thinkers) has helped create and continues to perpetuate a system that is so flawed and beyond repair their only response is to do away with it. And if good people who have fallen on hard times get eighty-sixed from the system, too bad. This is the prevailing attitude of hard core conservatives and it is causing the conservative movement to lose election after election.

In every group, there will be bad apples that will skew the message of the entire group. Seriously, we fight wars over that. So if we are willing to go over to other countries and risk the lives of our sons and daughters to rid their country of the bad apples and then set up a system that is fair, why can't we take that approach here in our own country with programs that have become too large and cumbersome? Why can't we take the entitlement apparatus and retool it? In the past we have tweaked it rather than retooled it and that was done based on the viewpoint of whatever party was occupying the White House. So if we tell the lobbyists to take a month off and our politicians cancel their junkets and cocktail parties perhaps a plan can be devised to overhaul the system so it becomes more manageable and fair. It is not fair to just cut people off but it is fair to get rid of the the people who have made a career out of scamming the government.

Everyone knows that a nation's strength has a lot to do with how educated their citizens are. One of the times in my life when I needed a hand up I was offered a chance at a job training program and I snapped it up. It was a beautiful thing and it worked. I needed help and the government said they could help so through mutual understanding they helped me and I helped them. I became fully employed and paid my share of taxes. No worries. If they had said, like they do now, we will give you cash aid, medical benefits, food stamps and help with your rent and nothing is required in return, I could have been doomed to of a life of professional recipient. But I was raised differently. Not everyone is raised in the same way and if you offer that deal to a weaker minded individual he or she may accept it and surrender a possibly different future. It's like trying to get a heroin addict off heroin by giving him Methadone. And then that person gets lost in a system so large and convoluted that if you were to actually come up with a new plan that would help, you wouldn't be able to find him.

Historically, when America experiences an economic downturn of any magnitude it can usually be traced to something business or the government did. And at the center of it would be greed and/or a grab for power. Both of which are weaknesses in people just like whatever weaknesses caused a person to find themselves in a position to ask the government for help. Do we turn our backs on business and government? No. Instead, we fix them. Just as we need to fix our programs to help those who have fallen on hard times rather than punish them by just doing away with the programs. The only way to do this is if both sides of the political spectrum agree that there are people who need and deserve help. We need to have programs that are manageable so the task must be given to the individual states because the Federal government can create anything and manage nothing.

Every program has to have a decent job with a future as a goal. This means America must stop exporting industries in favor of profit because once people are educated and/or trained there has to be a job for them. I am not saying America has to return to the practice of isolationism but it does mean that we have to stop sending every job overseas in order to improve a bottom line. Imagine if GE kept a few more jobs here in America and then actually paid taxes what it would do for the economy.

We currently have so few viable alternatives for the chronically unemployed that we have created a new class of poor. The existing class of poor is already placing incredible pressure on the system so this new class is going to cause it to implode so we need to do something now. And it can't be as simple as extending unemployment benefits again. The question that has to be answered is, what are we going to do with these people? If you think that at some point the economy is going to recover enough to put everyone back to work you are blowing smoke up your own a*s. Since the Great Recession it is a different economy. Our economy is fluid if only because the advances in technology are so fast and furious

Conservatives and Liberals like to box up political designations so as to protect their respective territories. I am a voter who tends to think along conservative lines yet I don't recognize the thinking of today's headline grabbing conservatives. They are obviously taking the wrong approach because they keep losing elections. You can take polls all day long to find out whether the country thinks more conservatively or liberally but at the end of the day all that matters is who shows up at the polling booth.

Guys, it's a new world. Instead of Ozzie and Harriet we are seeing Modern Family. The conservative mindset has to be somewhere between the two. Why you refuse to make even the most obvious adjustments is beyond me. If a Ted Cruz or a Marco Rubio thinks their going to get the Hispanic vote, good luck with that one. If you think voters will appreciate a war hawk in the White House, good luck with that one. If you think every person in need of government help would never vote, good luck with that one. Wake up and smell something because you seem to be ignoring everything. You are adding new meaning to being out of touch. I am conservative enough to not be able to stomach most far left thinking but I cringe every time I see John McCain quoted.

A TENUOUS RELATIONSHIP

America's relationship with Israel has become tenuous under the Obama Administration. Foreign policy in its entirety under Obama is suspect but to allow our relationship with Israel to devolve into tit for tat is unacceptable. Would we choose as our allies the likes of Iraq and Afghanistan over Israel? If we need a presence in the Middle East to "protect American interests" we will find no better partner than Israel.

It was reported today by the Associated Press that comments were leaked about John Kerry's efforts to broker a peace between Israel and the Palestinian Authority that are attributed to the Israeli Defense Minister and they ain't flattering. Boo hoo. Cry me a river. Israel is the only friend in the region that will never forsake us. If you interpret American interests as defense only then we need Israel more than they need us. Our relationship with Israel is like having a pit bull in your backyard. If anyone in that region messes with us, Israel will have our back. Now many would say we have lined Israel's coffers with billions of dollars especially in the form of military assistance and weaponry. What do you think that's for? If we want and expect Israel to have our back we have to arm them. We arm Iraq and Afghanistan and they turn around and use the weapons on us by letting them get into the hands of the bad guys. Think about that. If you are a country in that region and you don't necessarily like the United States but when you look down the street and you see United States military jets parked at an Israeli airport you are going to think twice. And so if some official in the Israeli government calls us names, deal with it.

If you want to listen to glib politicians who are as dumb as the day is long (despite their Ivy League degrees) that's your problem. If they are so damn smart why can't they solve at least one problem? They don't solve any problems. All they do is stand watch over the problems we already have and they aren't good at that because we keep seeing new problems. I'm not making this up, just read the news. So if these same guys are getting their shorts in a bunch because some official in Israel decides not to kiss their ass, too bad. I don't like John Kerry either. It was my generation that fought in the Vietnam war while John Kerry consorted with Jane Fonda. I could not even support Kerry as a dog catcher but Obama, the foreign policy maestro, has him representing our interests worldwide. And lest we forget, on the other end we have Joe Biden soothing the jangled nerves of our Asian friends.

Where's Hillary when you need her?

AGAIN WITH THESE POLITICIANS

Not that we need anything additional to add to the litany of reasons why politicians are so abhorring but as of this morning we have one more. In an article today about Governor Chris Christie, his behavior was debated in the context of being a leader or a bully. Politicians, mostly Democrats, have been using the bully term and it is outrageous. By doing so they diminish the seriousness of the ever present, ongoing problem of bullying in America. In New Mexico this week a 12 year old boy came to school armed with a shotgun and shot an 11 year old boy and a 13 year old girl. It has been reported it was possibly a result of bullying. Children in all parts of America are committing suicide as a result of bullying. This is a serious problem people and we can't allow these mealy mouthed politicians to use this childhood tragedy for political expediency.

And they further diminish the seriousness of the problem by not doing enough to address it. They seem to be more concerned with people using the N-word than anything else. Politicians are notorious for name calling that's why it was so ironic albeit funny that the White House got so upset this week over the Israeli Defense Minister calling John Kerry unflattering names. Yet they don't utter a word whenever Florida Democratic Representative Alan Grayson opens his mouth.

And frankly I don't care what you guys call each other because I always consider the source but when you have depleted your standard list of derogatory terms that you feel compelled to use a term associated with tragic events happening to our children, I draw the line. Enough is enough. Shut your pie holes. Whatever you say doesn't make a difference anyway (check the polls). Leave the children out of it. I am sure you can come up with plenty of names to call Governor Christie without using the term bully.

THE FREE SPEECH THREAT

We have three more years of Obama and his lapdog Eric Holder shredding our right to free speech. He has already, and will continue, to add people to the Administration that support his views. Some of those people are in jobs that they will remain in because they are not a type of appointment that would end with the completion of his term. So they will remain there to continue their assault on free speech even if we elect a new president that is a fierce proponent of free speech. And that brings to light another problem. More so for those of us who are registered independents. If we don't want another democrat as president who fails to protect free speech are we doomed to elect a republican that will protect free speech but get us into another round of wars and further enrich large corporations?

Must we sacrifice one right to protect another? We have a right to free speech that is protected by the Constitution. But we also have a right to life, liberty, and the pursuit of happiness which is endangered by the involvement in every cause around the world even ones that are remote to our interests. Obama would like to change a lot of laws that he doesn't particularly favor. He does this by circumventing Congress with the use of Executive Order, padding his Administration with like-minded people, and by stacking the Supreme Court. Imagine if he could get the House of Representatives on his side by achieving a Democratic majority?

As an independent I have the freedom to not carry the party line. On some issues I am liberal, on some I am conservative, and on others I am somewhere in between. To me that is a comfortable position because my political thought process is not dictated by a particular party's platform. Of course, the dilemma it creates is that I am truly in a position to have to choose between the lesser of two evils. Someday, probably not in my lifetime, Americans will expand the diversity of their thinking which will accommodate a third party (independent or whatever) that will hold equal sway in the political process. Attempts have been made in the past but unfortunately failed.

But until then we are forced to accept right wing thinking versus left wing thinking and not much in between. So although I voted for Obama I did not see the free speech assault coming. Political naivete I suppose. I want out of these pointless wars because I have a kid in the Marines and if a republican is in the White House we will be in a war somewhere. So come 2016 the choice between Hillary (is there any doubt?) and whoever the Republican Party comes up with, I will be between a rock and a hard place with all the other independents.

The assault on free speech by liberal thinkers has me so scared I feel I will be forced to go with the war mongers controlled by the corporations. The assault on free speech begins with the words we use but ultimately the assault will gravitate to the thoughts we have. So the "word police" today are the "thought police" of tomorrow. Granted we are still a young nation by the world's standards but to be represented by only two political parties (I don't take the Libertarians seriously) is archaic. And the really frightening part is these two parties are becoming more and more entrenched in their thinking which holds no hope for the future that either party will move more to the center.

Meanwhile, I am going to go down the street and call the neighbor I don't like a name while I still can.

WHAT'S SO SURPRISING?

It was reported that Maria Conchita Alonso was asked to leave the production of Brava! For Women in San Francisco because of her support for a Tea Party candidate for Governor of California. A statement from the production company read "Of course she has the right to say whatever she wants. But we're in the middle of the Mission. Doing what she is doing is against what we believe." I am not an actor or a producer but as a layperson I always had the impression that actors take on roles of characters and, hopefully, are so convincing you wouldn't know they aren't that character. What am I missing here? What does it matter what people think or do in their personal lives if they are playing a character? I can only assume that the production company's position is if a potential theater goer finds out about Alonso's political views they would refrain from attending based on that. Wow!

The bottom line here is **everyone** discriminates and if you claim you don't, you're a liar. I am so tired of the hypocrisy and double standards practiced by the people who claim to champion the rights of the disenfranchised. It seems the favored approach to getting people to accept a particular kind of thinking is to use force through discrimination. Isn't this what happened to Alonso? The production company committed an act of discrimination based on her political views. Isn't that a double standard? I'm pretty sure it is. If the production company claims it is their right to not have her in the show they are essentially saying they have the right to discriminate.

If one group wants another group to accept their position and they do so by essentially saying if you don't we will find a way to f**k you over, how is that any better? If their complaint is we are not accepting them because they are different well...they are not accepting us because we are different. Two wrongs have never made a right. And what about diversity in thought? Isn't that what makes a people great? For instance if a gay person says I need to be diverse in my thinking which would allow me to accept their lifestyle couldn't I say they need to be diverse in their thinking allowing them to accept my traditional viewpoint. It makes no difference to me if a person is gay and I don't do anything to impinge on that, but do I have to accept it? To each his own, right? There are a lot of lifestyles I don't accept as well as a lot of cultural norms. I'm a free American. Soldiers have died for me to have that right and my kid is a soldier and another is about to become one. You may not believe in the military. If my child does and takes on the responsibility to protect your freedom would it be right to exclude your freedom because you don't believe in the military?

The point is, in America we have freedom of speech and

thought. It's called a democratic society protected by a Constitution. If I don't accept you that is my right. What is not my right is to keep you from the same freedom of speech and thought. And the way you live is not my business as long as it is within legal boundaries. So do your thing and I will do mine and don't retaliate against me if I don't really prefer the way you live.

UNACCEPTABLE BEHAVIORS

The disdainful behaviors of professional athletes are unacceptable as they would be for anyone. The difference in the professional athlete is they are celebrated by the masses in both fame and fortune. With that goes, or should, a certain responsibility. In all probability the problem is simply an outsized ego which is easily controlled. You would think that control would be a result of the athlete himself wanting to be viewed as a gregarious, thoughtful, hard working person deserving of the fame and fortune bestowed upon them by a grateful public. For whatever reason that is not the case.

The most recent spectacle was the rant by Seattle Seahawks player Richard Sherman. For those who don't follow sports it was after the NFC Title game which decided who would represent the NFC in the Super Bowl. When interviewed immediately after the game Sherman essentially lost it. In an extremely threatening tone for millions worldwide to view, he gangster'd up. He spoke disparaging remarks with a top of his lungs voice regarding the player from the other team that directly opposed him in the match up and reminded him and anyone else it is foolish to try to beat his team in a football contest. Children and their parents all over the world watched this. Countries across the globe in which we spend millions of dollars promoting the American image were left bewildered. The Commissioner of the NFL whose staff monitors the behavior of the players and coaches saw it but has not issued a statement as yet. The family of the disparaged player saw it, and I am sure, felt it.

Just like a politician who stepped in it, the player released a halfhearted apology probably at the urging of his coach, agent, and team owner. He apologized for how it impacted his fellow players but he reasserted his feelings toward the other player. That was not an apology but rather a CYA move. And the media went with it. The public didn't buy it just like they don't buy it when it comes from our politicians. The team should have issued a written statement regarding the situation and then hoped it would fade away. Unfortunately, players like Sherman do this intentionally. They push the envelope as far as they can. They have a relatively small fan base that is obsessed with them and they feed it with these behaviors. It inflates the players ego albeit for the moment because we know that in a few days there will be another similar kind of outburst.

The world loves its sports and its players. This is evident by the aforementioned fame and fortune heaped on them. They deserve more from the players they adore. But players who behave in a manner that belies any sense of professionalism aren't concerned with them because they know that no matter how disgusted a fan may be they will not be able to dislodge them from their perch. It is the same with actors and politicians. In fact, these two groups, by virtue of their irrational behaviors, served as a model for the same kinds of behaviors in professional athletes. We will still go to the movies and continue to vote the politician back in office and we will still watch sports. That begs the question, “Are we enablers?” It's a legitimate question. But nevertheless, I refuse to accept that this glorification of the sports world is so intoxicating that it would permanently alter normal behavior patterns. In other words, the players choose to behave in this manner.

We can't have government regulation (or shouldn't in a free society) of irrational behaviors so regulation has to be in-house. The product that the government, movie producers, and sports team owners put out there is one that rewards them handsomely. Politicians are granted a very comfortable lifestyle replete with money and power, thanks to the voters. Advertisers with their deep pockets pay extraordinary sums to professional sports teams and in turn they lavish incredible salaries on players, thanks to the consumer. Producers pay stars millions of dollars per picture, thanks to the movie goer. For those rewards we deserve, in the least, something respectful. If a politician hates the opposing party they should still show some respect because they represent all the people.

Actors make movies for everyone so it isn't appropriate to publicly say they hate one or more particular groups of people because they think differently than them. And sports stars make their money from the advertising dollars that are a direct result of consumer spending.

So without us you don't have what you have so show some respect and curb your mouth.

AN UNFORTUNATE BY-PRODUCT

The freedoms America enjoys are far greater than most. Many countries operating under the banner of democracy are not so free as us. It is why we are at a critical juncture in our young history and must be careful lest matters spiral out of control. The last two decades have revealed much about the state of our union. Tonight President Obama will deliver the State of the Union address to inaugurate 2014.

How he will address the nation is less important then what is actually taking place behind the scenes. To have the President of the United States conduct a broadcast that will be viewed and analyzed worldwide by countries both friend and foe at a time when Americans are realizing transparency in government is total bull s**t (regardless of party affiliation) is embarrassing.

Much is said in political circles about credibility with the current president leading the charge. What does it say to Americans and the rest of the world when our leader takes center stage and essentially lies? And does so with one of the most ineffective body of legislators ever, applauding his every remark. So disillusioned am I that I will be watching reruns of Duck Dynasty instead.

How do you truthfully expound on the virtues of

transparency while knowingly spying on Americans (and world leaders) in the most intrusive manner? How do you promote less government in your life while at the same time attempting to regulate the speech of free Americans? How do you champion participatory government while using the Justice Department and the IRS as attack dogs against those who would disagree with you? How do you sell a collaborative government to the people when you circumvent Congress with the use of Executive Orders? How do you reign in the free spending financiers enriching themselves at the expense of the taxpayer when you expand the National Debt to stratospheric levels? What matters to us taxpayers is not who screws us but the fact we are being screwed in the first place.

So unless you care not that the United States is flushing itself down the proverbial toilet, you will stand with those who would tell our politicians and their financiers to pound sand.

We don't need your crap!

BEING GAY IN SOCHI

It is incredible just how much of a dick Vladimir Putin is. The Winter Olympics are about to get underway in Sochi, Russia and Putin is more worried about gay people showing up than terrorists. Are Russian men caught in a time warp like Middle Eastern men? Do they really think the presense of gay people is going to bring the world as they know it, to an end? Have they ever actually talked to a gay person? I have found that apart from some of the harsh rhetoric designed to convince us straight people to join their cause to be recognized like everyone else, they are really nice people. Something you can't say about gangbangers or former KGB agents.

Putin has no problem threatening other countries from time to time or supporting monsters like Asaad or condoning some of the worst cooruption ever but when it comes to gay people something there scares the s**t out of him. I thought only punk rockers could scare Putin but it is really gay people that scare him. I can't believe this is just a macho thing because that is really taking it too far.

And the fact is there has always been the presense of gays in the Olympics but it wasn't known. In today's world when hiding the truth about yourself isn't popular you see the reality of the situation. I will even venture a guess that before the Winter Olympics were awarded to Russia, there was probably already a few gays living in Russia.

What scares me most about this kind of crap is not that Putin is a dinosaur, we all know that, but he is always in possesion of nuclear codes for the express purpose of launching a nuclear weapon. So when you examine Putin's thinking regarding issues like supporting treacherous dictators, corruption, and homosexuality it isn't a stretch to ask the question “What might this guy do if provoked?”

It scares the hell out of me.

PLEASE TELL ME YOU ARE KIDDING

Today in Wisconsin something happened that I will never understand. A collision occurred between common sense and the labor movement that resulted in injuries to every sensible American. A seventh (get that, seventh) grade teacher was fired "after receiving and viewing multiple pornographic and sexually inappropriate images and videos" while at work. Somebody give me a barf bag. After the union set their attack dogs on the school district they caved and gave the teacher a new position as a seventh grade teacher at another school and will award him back pay in the amount of approximately $200,000. WTF?

We have two serious problems here. One is we have an obvious deviant knowingly working as a seventh grade teacher who is so into porn he can't wait to get home to view it. He has to do it at school. And secondly, we have a labor movement that is so single minded and obsessed with protecting what few members they have left they are willing to compromise their value system. I say that with the assumption they have a value system. Union officials do have kids, right? Or maybe they don't have kids at this particular school because I am bewildered they aren't offended by this guy.

We know defense lawyers defend criminals all the time because it is the criminal's constitutional right but that isn't the case with unions. The union does not have to protect a member to the extent they did in this situation. Which is why the second problem is even greater even though the teacher sickens us to our stomachs.

There is a reason why a group that over the years has been consistently losing members to the point that in 2013 they only accounted for 11.3% of the total workforce can wield such power. The reason they maintain such strength despite their dwindling numbers is because they are the Democrat Party get out the vote machine. It is so obvious they might as well change their name to just that. And the machine is so vital to the Democrats that they will turn a blind eye to the other work they do like get this teacher what amounts to a gift. Again, I am assuming there are Democrats who are parents that this would actually bother them.

Unions have few members but lots of money and a powerful Washington lobby. They can buy a politician dinner and get him votes. Politicians covet the offices they run for because of the power and influence they offer. How they get there is not as important as getting there.

So if that means they have to partner with a group that isn't winning any prizes for moral and ethical behavior, so be it.

This is the state of our union.

THINGS AIN'T SO GOOD THIS TIME AROUND

Come on, man. You are making me regret my decision to vote for you. Actually, I was already regretting it. I am one of those Independents that made the decision to vote for President Obama. Although I lean conservative I wouldn't vote for John McCain if he ran for dog catcher. But that's another story. Obama's first term wasn't totally offensive to me. I know he leans socialist but in America talk of socialism is only talk. The rich would never let it happen. It's a stretch to call our current welfare system socialism. You can certainly call it generous and unmanageable but not socialistic. So if Obama wants to talk about inequality I don't care if it is only talk and thus far, it is.

My regret is the second term. Winning the second term was a testament to Obama's political acumen. He took his accomplishments of the first term and skillfully parlayed them into a second term. Don't you love Chicago. It is what he has done, and not done, in his second term that has pissed me off. In the first term he had some impressive accomplishments. Obama signed into law The Recovery and Investment Act which, despite the naysayers, went a long way to begin the job of repairing a broken economy. He got us out of Iraq. He found a way with the efforts of our brave men and women to find Bin Laden and kill him. He went after the crooked bankers and made them pay for their part in the economic collapse. He came up with the Affordable Care Act which still needs a ton of work but it is something when something was needed and the Republicans weren't going to do it.

Based on these accomplishments and still feeling the sting of the last term of the Bush Administration along with my lack of empathy with Romney, I gave my vote to Obama again. Now I am not so sure that was a good idea. I thought in Obama's second term we would see some Wall Street types and a few bankers go to jail but instead they bought their way out. He has upped his chatter about the inequality issue (he now calls it that because it sounds less offensive than income re-distribution). We are still in Afghanistan propping up one of the most corrupt leaders ever known to mankind. The Affordable Care Act is still a mess. We are still hearing suspicious answers regarding Benghazi. The National Debt has skyrocketed. The use of the Executive Order to circumvent Congress is way out of line. Foreign policy is a sham. He continues to wear a teflon suit. And Eric Holder still has a job.

I could go on but I won't. You get my point. A second term offers any president the opportunity to expand on his first term accomplishments. It is also an opportunity to secure a legacy that won't be scoffed at by future generations. Obama doesn't seem to be concerned about either.

Instead, he is all over the map and not necessarily in a good way. He continues to shift blame and not take any himself. His arrogance is unmanageable.

It seems such a waste because Obama is a smart guy. He found a way to become the first black president of the United States and we needed to go there. But he needs to climb down from his high horse and be a president for all the people and he should allow Congress to do their job (and Congress needs to do a better job).

He talked mightily about transparency and credibility so now is the time to come through.

CLINT EASTWOOD FOR PRESIDENT, OBVIOUSLY

The man is 83 years old. He should be, if he's not already, a hero to all seniors. The news today is he saved the life of a 50 year old man as he was choking on some food. Clint used the Heimlich Method to dislodge the offending food that was destined to take the man's life. Again, the man is 83 years old. If that doesn't make all us senior couch potatoes think twice about aging I don't know what will. Seriously though it is an example of a man defying age. He works hard, plays hard, and speaks his mind as we saw during the last presidential election. There is no slowing this guy down. If AARP was smart they would put this guy center stage as an example to all seniors.

He holds to traditional values and he is beholden to no man. He is not afraid to speak his mind and he speaks it truthfully. I know he is probably not the least bit interested but wouldn't it be refreshing to have someone like him in the White House? Our country could only improve from the state it is now in. I am glad Clint is in the place he is now in his life. Enjoy it Clint, you earned it.

DOES OBAMA EVEN LIKE SENIORS?

The Obama Administration has done nothing that I am aware of, for the senior community. He has provided lip service that any half-witted person would recognize but apparently AARP hasn't. Let us not forget all the years of contributions we have provided. Not only through our productivity, taxes and participation in defending America but also through our contribution of values that seem to hold little importance these days for this generation. Old school is a good thing although many of the youngsters today are missing that point.

Seniors have gotten a raw deal in America. Look at the senior populations in other countries and tell me they are not taken better care of. Granted the tax structures in some of those countries are bizarre (France?) which allows them to take better care of their seniors. But in America it has never been about having enough money to take better care of seniors but about how Washington and the States manage the money. There is so much waste that if you cut out only a small portion of it you could elevate the living standards of America's senior population to stratospheric levels. In many ways the government provides more to crackheads than seniors. That's a damn shame. And if some Republican wants to liken senior benefits to an entitlement program they have their heads up their a*s. After all we have done for this country, you owe us!

I just did my taxes. I used H&R Block, who does not give a senior discount, and I paid taxes to a do nothing government that also did not give a senior discount. How many crackheads paid taxes this year? No matter what AARP says this country is in a f**k seniors mode. I just read today that convicts can sign up for Obamacare and don't have to pay. I am being forced to sign up for Obamacare and as a single man 62 years old I will pay close to $400 for a plan that has an astronomical deductible. The only way this plan is going to help me is if I get a life threatening disease. Who's pulling who's chain here?

I can't even believe seniors have to pay taxes. I have a home mortgage write-off (some politicians are advocating doing away with that) and I still paid taxes. I made just over $42,000 last year. I worked two careers and 34 years to get that so in a reasonable person's mind that is not much. I don't get food stamps, Medicare, Section 8, cash aid or anything else. It is all me and I still have to pay taxes and nearly $400 a month for medical benefits. So just what the f**k has Obama, or any president for that matter, done for me?

I think I'm going to go out and smoke some crack.

PUTIN THE P.O.S.

I don't know about you but I am tired of this clown. The man needs to grow up and grow a heart. He will need the heart because he doesn't have a brain. Why the Russian people put up with him is beyond me. What redeeming value could they find in this bozo? To begin with he is ex-KGB. Everyone in the Soviet Union feared the KGB and then they put him in charge of the country. Why would you do that? The man is like a little boy with a fragile ego hence the unending acts of bravado, the latest being the tiger cub in Sochi. What is he trying to prove? That he's tough? A person with an entire military force at his disposal doesn't have to act tough, we will assume it.

The guy doesn't need toughness, he needs intelligence and that is what he lacks. He, of course, could surround himself with intelligent people but then he would feel threatened so instead he surrounds himself with like-minded sycophants. People he can control with relative ease. He runs the country apparently with the help of the Russian Mafia. He snatched up Edward Snowden to tap the reservoir of intelligence he stole from his home country. We just saw that in the last couple of days when Russia hacked into a phone conversation between US Assistant Secretary of State Victoria Nuland and the Ambassador to Ukraine Geoffrey Pyatt in which the Secretary referenced the European Union with a not so flattering remark. Putin is going to use Snowden like a used up whore and then toss him aside. He will be lucky to get out of there with his life.

Putin is trying to put on a show in Sochi which is his MO to deflect attention away from the heinous things he is doing like keeping alive the Syria massacre of innocent civilians, jailing dissidents, and running rough shod on the gay community in Russia. And there is word now that major acts of corruption occurred involving billions of dollars with the construction of the Olympic venue in Sochi. It has been said Putin's personal wealth is estimated to be $75 billion making him one of the world's wealthiest. How does an ex-KGB agent acquire that much money even if he is elected to lead his country? What is the salary of a Russian president? You do the math.

What the guy does in his own country really isn't my business but when the lame brained, worthless United Nations puts Russia on the Security Council then it effects you and me and every other world citizen. Whenever the countries that give a crap try to intervene in a crisis like what we currently see in Syria, Russia finds a way to stop us usually by the veto power they have as a member of the Security Council. Syria is the last military installation Russia has outside of its own country. Since after WWII Russia (then the Soviet Union) and the United States have had shared interests in the region so they aren't willing to give up that military bulwark in Syria.

For now Russia is just a huge pain in the ass of the United States but that doesn't mean things won't get out of control and it doesn't help when Americans like Snowden and Nuland embarrass us.

JUST HOW STUPID IS IRAN?

It was just reported that Iran has sent several warships close to U.S. Maritime borders. This is a first. And it is really f**king stupid. Iran's navy compared to our navy would be like comparing aircraft carriers to row boats. Iran is a dog with a big bark and no bite. Are they really so stupid they would f**k with us when we could obliterate them in a New York second? They may be.

They might as well do this s**t while the Democrats are in charge because once the Republicans gain control it will be just like the transfer of power from Jimmy Carter to Ronald Reagan (providing, of course, the Republicans can come up with another Ronald Reagan). It is still a risky provocation because if you get Barack Obama on a day when he is feeling like a real man he may send a drone their way. That is all it would take. We send a couple of drones and suddenly Iran has no more navy.

The world right now is full of s**t talkers and Iran, North Korea and Russia are the biggest. But they are still wimps compared to America. One of these idiots will push us to a point that even the liberals will be in favor of suspending the ridiculous rules (the ones the liberals came up with) that hamstring us when dumb-ass nations do this kind of crap. And at that point we are going to eat you up and crap you out like a bad lunch.

You are just a bunch of junkyard dogs with deflated egos and you think your pathetic attempt at pushing around the biggest, baddest country known to mankind is going to get you some kind of street cred. Well, you are wrong. You may be able to push Obama around but there are still a few politicians with balls that will force the issue if your stupid games get too serious.

Push that envelope you dumb f**kers and see what happens.

THIS AIN'T NO CONUNDRUM

Another item today among the "dumbest things Washington is doing" regards the question of whether or not the U.S. should whack an al-Qaeda member that is killing Americans overseas but happens to have U.S. citizenship. Correct me if I am wrong but didn't Obama's oath of office state something about protecting us from our enemies whether foreign or domestic? I'm pretty sure I am right but I know how Obama likes to re-write things even the Constitution. Since I know Obama wouldn't pick up a water pistol to defend anyone it doesn't mean he should force his cowardly ways on the good citizens of America.

They have first hand knowledge that this creep is planning an attack on American interests abroad, again. So the question is how many Americans is Washington going allow to die at the hands of this guy before they stop him? You are going to have to wait a minute because they are thinking about it. Chime in with the Jeopardy tune now because it could be awhile.

They say the difficulty in this decision "underscores the complexities of President Barack Obama's new stricter targeting guidelines for the use of deadly drones." Well who the f**k asked him to come up with that? I don't recall ever getting anything in the mail asking for my opinion which, by the way, would be to whack the guy. And the information is bogus that he is a "suspected" member of al-Qaeda because we know he is otherwise we wouldn't be having this conversation.

The real problem is too many rules. Liberal Americans operate "rule factories" that churn out rules that are designed to move us closer and closer to socialism and the wussification of America. If a known killer walks up to you in the street and declares he is going to kill you, would you first check his freakin' passport. No, a conservative would kill the guy himself and a liberal would cry out for help and then ask his savior to go easy on the killer. I am only stating the facts here that have been collected for years through observation.

First of all, if it is a country that does not allow military action on its soil then it is not a country friendly to the U.S. although we are probably giving them foreign aid. We know this country is not going to allow us in because four, not three, not two, not one but four U.S. officials said this. Memo to U.S. officials: we don't believe anything you say so it doesn't matter if four or forty officials say something.

If it were a friendly country we should be able to go in there, join forces with them, and take the guy out. It's called a collaborative effort. So this is probably a country that really f**king hates us if they won't let us in and won't do it for us. It's probably Pakistan. Obama has said he wants to “calm anger overseas regarding our drone activity” (I'm sure there was an apology in there somewhere) but frankly a lot of us don't really care what others think when it comes to a life or death situation.

So in a nutshell, there are people in the Middle East who hate us and wish we were dead and there is a guy over there that we know is already killing us and looking for a way to kill more of us and we are sitting around talking about it.

Oy vey!

A TRAVESTY OF JUSTICE

Today an American Judge and Judicial System dishonored a fallen hero. Brian Terry was a Border Patrol Agent murdered by a drug dealing illegal alien. He was given 30 years for it. It was a plea bargain to avoid the death penalty. Those plea deals are usually for life in prison with no parole. I am convinced Mexico intervened and played a role in this ridiculous sentence. This is the kind of sentence a murderer in Mexico would get. So because the murder was committed with a weapon from the Fast and Furious debacle of the Justice Department, the sentence was in large part to appease angry Mexican politicians that are still upset that we fed guns to the cartels. No American gets that deal.

Our government used Brian Terry to regain favor with the Mexican government. The reason our government is kissing the ass of the Mexican government has everything to do with business and how much money the corporate world makes from that business. And since we know the corporate world owns the government it doesn't take a genius to figure this out. It is especially plausible when you look at the Fast and Furious program. That was sheer stupidity perpetrated by highly educated men and women in government. Not even a crackhead would do something so stupid. What were they thinking? Only an idiot doesn't understand the nature of the relationship between government and business.

Everything begins and ends with the economy. It is what separates the great nations from the not so great nations. Government and business must have this relationship but beyond that it has to be a relationship devoid of undue influence. Unfortunately, we don't have that here in America because we allow lobbying by large corporations and industry trade groups. This is, and always will be, the great divide. A government can't maintain a relationship that creates an imbalance between it and it's people but that's what they do when they allow the kind of influence they allow from business. And this is what happened to Brian Terry. The Mexican government didn't really care about the arms from the U.S. falling into the hands of the cartels. The cartels were already one of the most heavily armed criminal organizations with the most sophisticated weaponry.

This is probably more about Mexico saving face in the International Community because our overzealous Justice Department had the audacity to violate their sovereignty. Mexico is a business ally only, they are not a military ally with anyone. Allied forces go to war and Mexico stays home. I imagine there is more trade going south then coming north which means we have a lot to lose if Mexico gets overly pissed. So the leverage Mexico has with us is business and nothing else because we don't need them for anything else.

No matter the business dealings America may have with Mexico they have both stooped too low by using Brian Terry as a pawn. Brian Terry was a hero and should be treated as such.

WHAT WERE YOU THINKING?

The winning of the mayorship in San Diego by a Republican is more significant than most see right now. Despite a last minute endorsement from the President himself it didn't sway San Diego voters. This doesn't bode well for Democrats in the upcoming mid-term elections if the President can't help even a mayoral candidate. Also, it is reported that organized labor pumped upwards of $4 million into the candidacy of Democrat David Alvarez. That's a lot of change for a mayoral race. The Democrats decided to stand on a political platform of a singular issue which in many minds is the tired issue of labor that we need to raise the minimum wage and fix the poor neighborhoods. Middle America is already disgusted with Obama over this kind of political action because it presupposes Middle America is doing just fine. Middle America is still reeling from high unemployment numbers and as insensitive as it may seem they are more concerned with themselves than the poor right now.

Until the debacle that is Bob Filner, San Diego had not elected a Democrat to the mayor's office in two decades. Talk about missing a golden opportunity. Why they chose Filner is beyond me especially when the Democrats knew of accusations of inappropriate behavior. Knowing the candidate field was weak why couldn't they come up with someone better than the arrogant fool Filner? After Filner totally screwed things up San Diego realized why they don't elect Democrats to the mayor's office.

This is why the local Democrat Party turned the mayor's race into a crap shoot. They used Alvarez knowing he didn't have a chance. And then they sent him out there with a message they knew wouldn't resonate. This was unfair to Alvarez and to the Hispanic Community because San Diego could have realized their first Hispanic mayor. There is a number of prominent Hispanics who could have won this race the first time. Lorena Gonzalez certainly comes to mind.

The Los Angeles Times is soft peddling the result of this mayoral election because they won't acknowledge the truth. The truth is the Democrat Party, along with Labor, blew this one. Obama's coat tails are not what they were after the his first election. After the second election a lot of what he is doing is, in the least, questionable. He seems more concerned about his legacy than anything else.

As a resident of San Diego county I would like to see the city of San Diego pick itself up and get on the right track. Regardless of who is now the mayor I think San Diegans are going to have some high expectations and deservedly so.

REALLY?

I am not a fan of NASCAR although it seems its fans are as dedicated as those of us who are football fans. In following sports I do read articles now and then about the happenings around the sport of race car driving. One article that recently garnered headlines seemed curious because it was an article that would have been more likely many years ago. It came straight from the Petty family which seems to indulge in the petty.

For some reason Richard Petty, the godfather of racing, felt a need to disparage Danica Patrick in an interview. It was just last year that Danica endured the same sort of thing from the son, Kyle Petty. This latest remark from the patriarch officially proves the Petty family is a bunch of dinosaurs. In the interview Richard Petty said the only way Danica Patrick is going to win in the Sprint Cup Series is if all the other drivers stayed home. To begin with this can be said about 50% or more of the other drivers since this isn't the Pro Bowl of racing. But what clearly irks the "stuck in time" Petty is the popularity of Danica and the fact she is a woman. It's obvious. Coming from a generation not known to champion the cause of feminism the elder Petty must be having a tough time adjusting to a female race car driver going up against men (and refusing to wear an apron while doing it).

But in true Danica fashion she handled it with the kind of class we wish we all had. And it is the reason she has done so much for the sport (except win, I guess) and why the Petty family should be grateful. I never gave racing a second thought until she came on the scene and piqued the interest of so many. And the fact is, she is prettier than Richard Petty. She races well enough to compete, has brought untold numbers of female fans into the professional racing family, and continues to bring attention to the sport from those whose lives do not revolve around it. Which makes her a very capable ambassador of professional racing.

Now is that so bad Richard?

LET'S BE HONEST

Americans are bullies. Seriously. Not only are we bullies, we are major bull sh**ters because we go to great lengths to portray the bully problem as if is is isolated to some area in our lives like American schools. Currently, we are all up in arms because a story emerges almost daily that a tragedy has occurred to a 13 year old as a result of being bullied in school. It's all over the media and politicians are scrambling to create laws concerning it. This only shows how we have not only ignored this problem for years but we have actually made it worse.

Whether it is the President of the United States or Richie Incognito or Martin Bashir or Alec Baldwin or lobbyists, we are bullies. This is not something new here in America. Not only are we bullies but we display it constantly in so many ways and we make sure it is seen worldwide. Even though I am talking specifically about America right now it is obvious bullying is a problem worldwide and too often is deadly. What is a Vladimir Putin or a Assad Bashar or Mahmoud Ahmadinejad? They are bullies.

So how do we stop the bullying that is happening to our children if the examples we set make it seem that bullying is okay? The first thing we need to do is to more clearly define bullying. And we need to start at the top with the most recognizable positions in the world, the Presidency of the United States and the United States Congress. President Obama has said he will use his phone, pen, veto power and the Executive Order to get what he wants if Congress won't give him what he wants. On a daily basis Congress stops legislation in its tracks not based on what the people want but instead it is about political ideology. Just ask someone who received their last unemployment check.

Both the President and Congress are using bully tactics but call it negotiation. Are you f**king kidding me? The NFL is showcasing bullies to millions worldwide and say it is part of the strategy used in Professional Football. So if Richie Incognito says horrendous things to Jonathan Martin off the field or Richard Sherman calls out Michael Crabtree after the game, it is a strategy. Are you f**king kidding me? If Alec Baldwin puts himself out there as a celebrity and therefore photographers everywhere want a piece of his life, it is okay to threaten violence against them? Are you f**king kidding me? If Martin Bashir doesn't like the political thinking of Sarah Palin it is okay to tell her to eat s**t on national television? Are you f**king kidding me? If a trade group uses its vast resources of money to whine and dine politicians and then tell them how to vote, is that fair to the American public? Are you f**king kidding me?

And these are but a few examples. Examples we are all aware of but seem to ignore. How do you ignore Kanye West bullying people in the media and at concerts? He does it as a strategy to keep the attention on his career. Hollywood and the recording industry love it because when Kanye enters into another diatribe the connection is immediately made to the Kardashians. So his record label and the producers of the Kardashians get a boatload of free publicity.

When well known people engage in bullying it is a confirmation in the minds of the young and impressionable (as well as established grownups who follow the lead of others) that these tactics are okay when, in fact, they are bully tactics. The ones who perpetrate these deplorable acts can call it whatever they want but at the end of the day it is bullying.

So if we ever intend to protect our children from the bullies of the world we must start at the upper echelon of society where they freely commit acts of bullying and disguise it with words like negotiation, publicity, strategy, or whatever other bull s**t name they want to give it.

It is still bullying.

SAY WHAT YOU MEAN

President Obama has such a difficult time with words. He is so concerned about offending someone that he comes up with the most unoffensive way to say something. A case in point is an article today regarding our relationship with Uganda (who sucks at the American teat) and the new anti-gay law that "includes a provision of life in prison for aggravated homosexuality." The response from the White House was that it would "complicate" our relationship with Uganda if they enact the new law. As a service to my country I will help translate what I hope the President truly meant. "If Uganda enacts this new, incredibly stupid law it would totally f**k up the relationship with the United States and they will be cut off from the nearly quarter of a billion dollars we give them every year." How's that?

Mr. President, either you are going to protect the rights of the gay community or not. I am not part of the gay community but I am part of the every human being has rights community. You can't tell the LGBT Community in America you support their cause and then turn around and give over $250 million dollars in annual aid to another country that wants to jail for life a person who happens to choose a gay lifestyle. I believe that's called hypocrisy. We already do business with too many countries suspected of detrimental treatment of their citizenry.

Let's face it, China is our banker and how are women and gays treated in Saudi Arabia? As twisted as it may be we are forced sometimes to do business with the likes of China and Saudi Arabia but Uganda? Really? Uganda does nothing for the U.S. unless Washington admits to having an interest in Uganda's oil. But to admit that they would also have to admit that despite Uganda's terrible record on human rights and the despicable legislation that targets gays, they are willing to do business with them and continue to give them free money that rightfully belongs to American taxpayers.

At some point Washington needs to place human values over business and military needs unless they are of an absolute need and in the case of Uganda, they are not.

CENSORSHIP IN AMERICA

Since Barack Obama became president we have seen an attack on free speech that we haven't seen in decades in this country. This should scare the bejeezus out of every American.

Maybe it is because we elected a black socialist from the Democratic party and across the country liberals have taken elective offices in large numbers and every wealthy/well known celebrity, athlete, activist, businessman, etc. that has liberal leanings has taken advantage of their soapbox. Whatever it is, the attack on free speech is evident every day in the news. In the last couple of weeks we have seen a high profile case with Phil Robertson of Duck Dynasty fame professing his beliefs regarding homosexuality to a teacher in Ohio who made the remark "We don't need another black president." A & E suspended Robertson and the school board suspended the teacher.

Now I have never said the things these guys said but I want to continue my right to do so if I choose. I have a kid in the Marines ready to fight and die for that right and not just for me but for you as well. It started as political correctness and has snowballed from there almost exclusively at the behest of liberals. And Barack Obama with his admitted socialist leanings has championed the plight of blacks especially with his remark to the world about Trayvon Martin.

Everything I have said so far is factual. If my remarks are factual and presented in the course of a civilized discussion why wouldn't it be okay in a country that was founded on the right to free speech? Because the liberals are using political correctness as a vehicle to get to where they want to go which is the regulation of our thoughts and actions. It's not just that they don't want me to refer to our president as a black socialist. They know he is but they don't want me to call him that. But even though they know he is and they don't want me to use that “label” they want me to accept that he is black and that he has socialist leanings otherwise I am a racist, neanderthal, far right wacko, or any of the many names they come up with to disparage those who do not think like them.

I am a white conservative and now a registered Independent that voted for Barack Obama, twice! I left the Republican party after the debacle of the George Bush presidency and I couldn't bring myself to support the McCain/Palin ticket. I am a pensioner that makes less than fifty thousand dollars a year which is why I am of no interest to the Republican Party. I support a woman's right to abortion and gay rights not because I believe in it but because it is their right. If we go to war I believe we should have no rules and obliterate the enemy and come home. I believe in the death penalty even for child molesters. As you can see I am all over the political map. If you can't stomach my all over the map beliefs, too bad. It is my right.

Although I voted for Obama twice I have to admit he pulled the wool over my eyes. When he was first elected he impressed me. He sacred me a little bit with his income redistribution beliefs but I knew they would go nowhere in our free market society. At the time of the first election the world pretty much knew the financial industry was the true culprit behind the collapse of the economy through the use of derivatives. John McCain refused to accept that and continued to blame the American worker for getting in over their heads. He also likes to go around the world kicking everybody's ass who doesn't agree with him. If my kid is going to fight in a war it better be a righteous one. And then, bless her heart, he named Sarah Palin as his running mate. Sarah Palin is qualified to be a feisty mayor of a small town, just like Joe Biden is. Neither one is qualified to be the President of the United States.

So it was truly a lesser of two evils situation and in this election the Democrat was the lesser evil. Once Obama got up and running I was impressed with enough of what he was doing that I could deal with the things he did that I didn't agree with. I liked the draw down of our troops because we weren't prosecuting the war in the way we should so it was going the way of the Vietnam conflict. He went after the bankers who I now consider to be low life thugs in designer suits. He pushed for Wall Street reform. He bagged Osama Bin Laden. He pushed for greater advances in stem cell research. He created the Affordable Care Act.

But he also did some things I didn't like. I wanted the Affordable Care Act but not in the way it was finally rolled out. The Republicans have no interest in helping the poor or seniors so at least Obama is doing something in that area. He just didn't do it well. His grasp of foreign policy is suspect. We are making mistakes all over the globe. He has failed to rein in the oil companies who are thugs just like the banks. He circumvents the Congress every chance he gets. He ignores State's rights. He allows the NSA to spy on everyone. But worst of all he is the leader in the effort to suppress free speech. When he became president liberals went hog wild in their desire to make this country walk to the beat of their drum. Everything they did was right and what everyone else did was wrong. Meanwhile our president, who represents all citizens, has done nothing to abate their efforts.

You can create policies that I don't like and I will accept them as any good citizen would. But if you start f**king with my constitutional rights I have to draw the line. Especially since I have a kid in the military and another one about to join. If some dirt bag like Phil Robertson wants to voice his weird opinions, he can do that. If some teacher in Ohio chooses to use the wrong words, he can. I don't like it anymore than the liberals but it is still their right. And what is worse is the liberal community's selective manner in which they demonize the "offenders." Charlie Sheen, Steve Martin, Joe Biden, Al Sharpton, Bill Maher all get a pass but Phil Robertson doesn't or the teacher in Ohio doesn't. The word police can practice a double standard and the pushers of tolerance can be intolerant and it is okay.

The president comes out and says Trayvon Martin could be his son. That amounts to an endorsement of the case as being racist when there was no evidence of racism just evidence of George Zimmerman committing what amounts to manslaughter because he is the world's biggest dumb-ass. And how is it that person condemning what they view as intolerant speech does so by using what should be intolerant speech? The media, for some absurd reason, chose to highlight Charlie Sheen's twitter rant about Phil Robertson. In that rant he disparages old people. Charlie your dad is an old person! As an immoral dirt bag (and recognized as such worldwide) you have the gall to criticize another? Clean up your own back yard first Charlie.

So this stuff goes way beyond censorship by approaching a fascist attitude. It's not just the words we say it is about what we think and feel. You liberals all think the rest of us should speak, think, feel, and act the way you do. Because your way is the right way. Or so you think. A lesson was learned, I hope, when the Phil Robertson thing backfired.

Fascism does not allow for diversity. Groups are turning to the government, and Obama welcomes them, to get their way. They will use their vote, buying power, and access to the media to get what they want.

IF THE TRUTH BE TOLD

With the recent developments in Fallujah conservatives are coming out of the woodwork to play the blame game. They are backed by many of the military high command who are lost unless they live every waking moment in an active war zone. We all painfully remember how tragic Fallujah was in regard to military personnel lost. But if our battle plan is to preserve areas in which we won hard fought victories then we would be in the back yards of countries all over the world.

The Iraqi forces are like a tragic version of the Keystone Cops. We spent too many lives and billions of taxpayer dollars to train these knuckleheads and it was all a waste. They have reverted to the way they did things in the past because everything we taught them was forgotten 20 minutes later. These guys can never be bona fide soldiers.

The kind of fighter they are is the only kind of fighter they can be. Dumb as a rock and willing to do anything even killing women and children and cutting off the heads of their enemies. That's how they roll. Yet we go in there all sophisticated, trained at the best schools and loaded with money and we expect these guys to become like us? Are you f**king kidding me? That's like taking criminals in America, putting them on probation, drug testing them and using the flavor of the month behavioral science to try to fix their lives. It doesn't work. And it sure isn't going to work in a foreign country in which the customs and traditions in no way resemble ours.

These people are beyond repair. There is far too many elements to their hate. They hate each other, they hate Jews, they hate other religions, they hate other sects of their own religion, they hate their personal lives, they hate their leaders, and they hate Americans. And that is the short list.

The fact is we need to devise another approach to protect American interests (I'm still trying to figure what that term means). We have also heard the terms core interests, business interests, in the interest of America, the list goes on. I realize the world needs oil and we need to guard against some whack job with a dirty bomb and keep in check the little tyrants of the world but lets not do it in a haphazard way. There has to be other ways to tell the Iraqis that if they bring their s**t out of their country and try to deposit it in ours we will flush their entire country down the toilet. We can begin by just ignoring them. Then we get our friends to ignore them. At some point they will come around. We see it now in Iran and at some point North Korea will have no choice but to ask for help. If they don't it is because the hate will finally do them in.

WHY BOTHER?

The UN has issued yet another report about another atrocity and it begs the question "Why bother?" The UN and the richest and most powerful nations aren't going to do anything about it. They never do. Oh they might offer some lip service but that will be the extent of it. There will be no follow through. Just ask yourself "What problems in the world has the UN and the richest and most powerful nations actually solved?" I can't think of any. As far as I know s**t is falling apart all over the world. Our children and grandchildren are going to inherit a frickin' mess that is being created right now!

The world is full of smart guys in charge that can't find their ass with two hands. Syria, Iran, North Korea, and India (where rape is a sport) are at the head of a list of f**ked up countries and nothing is being done. But if you survey the people who are supposedly charged with the responsibility of fixing s**t or the people who should take it upon themselves to help remedy the situation (because they are in a position to do so) some things stand out. They all have tons of money, power and fame. And for those with the least amount of money among them, power and fame will lead to wealth at some point. It's a process.

The unfortunate bottom line is that nothing gets fixed. Syria keeps killing its citizens, Iran is doing their typical let's bull s**t the world routine, North Korea is doing horrific things to their people and if you are a woman you may not want to travel to India. The world has shown it cannot police itself. We see evidence of this every day and it is the very people who rely on leadership to protect them that are being victimized. The recent revelations outlined in the UN report on North Korea are starting to make the Syrian tragedy pale in comparison. These tragedies will get reviewed, discussed, and findings will be presented while all along more innocent people will perish.

So is this all for show? We have to wonder because if a world body like the UN along with the G8 nations are rendered impotent in light of these atrocities perhaps it is nothing more than a show when they step up and declare something must be done. Well, we aren't that gullible. We know you are not getting the job done although you are equipped to do so.

Personally, I think the “business” of the world is what's getting in the way. We are a global economy that has to stay in balance so only so much attention and resources can be diverted. Even if people are dying.

www.ingramcontent.com/pod-product-compliance
Lightning Source LLC
Chambersburg PA
CBHW060240290526
45789CB00001B/129

9781499761412